Kyle Beveridge has written ⟨...⟩ invaluable wisdom and perspective on investing, and more importantly, the most important question of all time. We must all answer about our eternity! Highly recommended read.

—BRIAN S. WESBURY
Chief Economist, *First Trust Advisors L.P.*

I so enjoyed this story of wealth-building through a foundation of hard work, ethical practices, and biblical principles. This is exactly how I built my business and grew my personal net worth, so I can attest to the fact that Kyle Beveridge's ideas work. One suggestion alone—for business-owners, young people just getting started, and those facing retirement years—is worth the price of this book. Read it and find out for yourself!

—JENNY PRUITT
Executive Chairman, *Atlanta Fine Homes*
Sotheby's International Realty

I enjoyed the combination of storytelling and applicable financial principles that can help anyone build a wholistic net worth.

—BEN SNYDER
Lead Pastor, *CedarCreek Church*

This book has incredible insight into the basic fundamentals that are needed for a healthy financial foundation. These writings will encourage you to invest in your now, as well as your eternity. I highly recommend this for people of all ages.

—MICAH PELKEY
Pastor, *Storyside Church*

Kyle Beveridge gives you insight from his personal journey of catapulting his business into twenty times its original value. You will be inspired, equipped, and activated to grow your own net worth. "Hey, it's your money," you will be helped to be a player and not just a payer.

—MICKEY ROBINSON
Author, *Supernatural Courage, Falling Into Heaven*

HOW TO BUILD YOUR TRUE NET WORTH

HOW TO BUILD YOUR TRUE NET WORTH

In a Post-Pandemic World

KYLE BEVERIDGE

To my mother, Mary Elise (Weise) Beveridge,
who invested in me her steadfast love
and a desire for diligence, a devotion to duty,
and a determination to succeed in life,
while storing up treasures in heaven.

and

To my wife, Kimberly,
who has supported me for over forty-five years,
and who continues to teach me
the joy of kindness, forgiveness, and frugality...
not to mention how to control my judgmental spirit!

"Historical evidence speaks with a single voice on the relation between political freedom and a free market. I know of no example in time or place of society that has been marked by a large measure of political freedom, and that has not also used something comparable to a free market to organize the bulk of economic activity.

Because we live in a largely free society, we tend to forget how limited is the span of time and the part of the globe for which there has ever been anything like political freedom: the typical state of mankind is tyranny, servitude, and misery.

The nineteenth century and early twentieth century in the Western world stand out as striking exceptions. Political freedom in this instance clearly came along with the free market and the development of capitalist institutions."

—MILTON FRIEDMAN
Author of *Capitalism and Freedom*

Remember the LORD your God, or it is he who gives you the ability to produce wealth, and so confirms his covenant [with you]. (Deuteronomy 8:18)

CONTENTS

INTRODUCTION

"KYLE!" MY MOTHER would call out to me. "It's time to clean your room!"

More often than not, the response from my former rebellious, spoiled self would be, "I can't, Mom."

Her attempts to mold me into a caring, compassionate, and obedient son and servant of God never waned. So, inevitably, I would hear some other instruction, such as, "Kyle, would you feed the cat and empty the litter box?"

"Can't, Mom!" I would shout back from my bedroom.

But she was not to be defeated. "Kyle, how about weeding the flower beds out by the split-rail fence?"

By now, you know my stock answer.

Each time I used the word *can't,* she delivered what was more a grim warning than a stinging rebuke: "*Can't* died in the poorhouse!"

I detested that statement. It made the hair on the back of my neck stand straight up! If there was anything I feared more than the dreaded chores, it was the possibility of ending up in the "poorhouse," although it was pretty unlikely in those days.

Living on a two-hundred-acre farm with my mother and father, who was making a six-figure annual income and driving luxury cars at the time, the prospect of the poorhouse did seem remote. Still, the specter of "going broke" haunted me. Maybe that is why I bypassed my original career path as a farmer who loved watching things grow. That idea fell by the wayside when it became apparent that you couldn't make enough money by farming alone to support two families on just two hundred acres.

After graduating college, I even considered becoming a history teacher. But when my dad retired from his insurance agency, where he had racked up an enviable list of accomplishments, including the Million-Dollar Round Table, he turned the business over to me. It wasn't long before I found that helping people grow their net worth was equally satisfying—although there was the occasional "drought" when the stock market would take an unexpected plunge.

Take the year 2020, for instance. I am writing this book in the midst of one of the fastest stock market crashes in history, dating back to 1802. These 219 years cover the period when the most accurate financial data was recorded. In a few days, the Dow Jones industrial average, the S&P 500, and the NASDAQ fell 30% after all three indices had just set all-time record highs. That triggered a seismic shift in the global economy. Add in a pandemic, and you have a recipe for disaster!

That's where I hope this book comes in.

For the past forty-two years, it has been my privilege to counsel several hundred individuals and more than one hundred fifty small business owners. Therefore, within these pages, you will find information on building your net worth through investments in a variety of industries, tips on diversification, hints on building a successful business even in a plunging economy, preparing for retirement so you won't outlast your money, leaving a legacy of prosperity, and looking forward to the future, both earthly and eternal—no matter what comes our way.

Throughout history, every society has had its caste system—nobility vs. peasants—permeating every culture and race on virtually every continent. This has been true up until the founding of the capitalistic philosophy, which allows any person who works, studies, and applies their God-given talents to the best of their ability to reach the pinnacle of their career and create wealth.

I once heard of a college professor who announced to his class that their next project would be a study on socialism—the polar opposite of capitalism. When he asked how many in the class believed in socialism, they all raised their hands.

"Okay, class," he said, "we're going to do an experiment next session. Come prepared tomorrow with some money in your pocket."

When they reconvened the next day, he asked the students how many had money with them. Several raised their hands, including John, who said that he had a twenty and some change. Several others admitted they had brought no money to class.

"John, give your twenty-dollar bill to Melissa," ordered the professor. "She doesn't have any."

"No way!" John protested. "I worked for this money! I'm not giving it to someone who doesn't work!"

When the professor insisted, John reluctantly parted with his twenty.

This went on for some time, with those who had money giving it to those who had none. Fiery arguments broke out in the class.

"My parents keep me on a budget! I can't give away my spending money!"

"I worked all summer for this money, and I have books to buy!"

While those without money admitted they didn't work or that they had already blown their allowance for the week, a lot of yelling and insults ensued.

Eventually, the professor called for silence, then announced, "Welcome to socialism, class!"

When he took another poll, the whole group voted *against* socialism.

• • •

The Declaration of Independence, along with the Bill of Rights, Rule of Law, and Land Rights, formed the foundation for the society with the greatest potential for wealth creation ever known. That society is the United States of America—and unless we are wise, we are in danger of losing the freedoms we hold so dear.

While there are many books on the subject of money management and investing, my hope is that, in addition to providing some fundamental facts in light of our present economic dilemma, I can point you to the only Source of true and lasting wealth—our Maker and the Owner of "the cattle on a thousand hills."

In my personal Bible study, as I have searched for wisdom to advise my clients, I have been amazed to discover how often this issue is discussed. For example, while *love* is mentioned 714 times and *faith* only 268 times, *wealth, money, giving,* and *possessions,* etc. are mentioned 2,172 times![1] Therefore, throughout this book, you will find selected passages that will reveal the final word on the matter, promising eternal returns on your investment.

A very wise woman put it this way: "As Christians, we are partners and stockholders in the kingdom of God. We have ownership with our Father. This brings unlimited resources that are untapped. We also have spiritual currencies available to us. After all, we are joint heirs with Jesus Christ. That alone is mind-boggling! This is why you need to PRAY BIG. Don't pray small but ask for what you need. Uncap your rightful inheritance and use your spiritual currencies. It's easier than you think."[2]

I agree. So, I have chosen to write this book, weaving together three elements: personal stories of my search for significance, both failures and favor; the five building blocks of our successful investment business; and biblical principles that will help you develop the key to your own success, both spiritual and financial.

So, don't forget! You are made in the image of our Creator God, who wants to unleash in *you* the creative ability to build true wealth. Therefore, I invite you to join me on my journey to discover the secret of creating a net worth that will last a lifetime— and beyond. May my experiences encourage, inspire, and motivate you to press on in the face of seemingly insurmountable problems, predicaments, and even global pandemics.

Chapter 1

A TIME TO TAKE STOCK

There is a time for everything,
and a season for every activity under heaven:
A time to be born, and a time to die;
A time to plant, and a time to uproot;
A time to tear down and a time to build up....
A time to keep and a time to throw away.
(Ecclesiastes 3:1–3, 6)

SNOHOMISH COUNTY, WASHINGTON STATE, USA. January 20, 2020. The date the first case of a novel virus, COVID-19, was reported in a 35-year-old man who had recently returned from a trip to visit family in Wuhan, China. The rest is history, a history that is still being written.

That virus infected not only millions of people as it raced around the globe, but it infected our national economy. With the Center for Disease Control mandating quarantine to keep the virus from spreading, businesses closed and thousands upon thousands of employees were laid off. Of course, the stock market (i.e., the Dow, the S & P 500, and the NASDAQ) reacted to this unprecedented event and plunged several percentage points in thirty days, continuing to see-saw with each new report from the media.

Just when we thought things could not get any worse, they did. After the financial meltdown came the horrific racial incident—the videotaped murder of a black man by a police officer—that set off protests across the nation, erupting in violence and destruction of property, including businesses that had taken their owners decades to build. Still, no one who viewed the footage of that dreadful sight will ever forget the victim's last words: "I...can't...breathe."

Well, it's time we all pushed the pause button. To pause and reflect. To take stock of where we are and where we need to be in these turbulent times. Come reminisce with me...

• • •

Butler, Ohio. Population: 993. A real-time Mayberry, U.S.A.

Surrounded by lush, fertile fields and rolling countryside flanking the Clear Fork River that merges with the beautiful Mohican River, winding its way through North Central Ohio, Butler was the small town where I was born in November 1955, and where I grew up. In all these years, the town hasn't changed much, while most everything else has. A few miles away is the city of Mansfield, Ohio, once known as a thriving manufacturing center, producing everything from cars to gas and electric stoves. But I was a country boy, and later when my family purchased a two-hundred-acre farm, I was elated. Loved the open air and catching fireflies in the summer and watching things grow.

In the aftermath of World War II, the decades of the '50s and '60s were relatively peaceful—with the exception of the Korean and Vietnam Wars—as Americans turned from the war effort to chase their dreams. In my teens, I worked hard on the farm and played hard, running track and cross country for my high school and making it to the regionals, setting two records—one that lasted twenty-five years. As my good pal Ted Schluter used to say, I was "better than most, but not as good as some." It was a time when folks feared God and respected the flag, and prayer was still part of the public square.

With life in slow motion during these idyllic days, who would have imagined that several years down the road, things would turn sour almost overnight? My dad, who was absorbed in building his life and health insurance business during my youth, missed many of my own pivotal life moments—especially the athletic events where I seemed to shine the most. With his business smarts, though, he might have been able to predict the economic storms that have rolled in recently. Unfortunately, he is no longer with us, and I have some regrets...

REARVIEW MIRROR

Some have said that looking too long in the rearview mirror is a negative. Best not to look back, they caution. Just move on. Can't change what happened in the past anyway. Really? What about growing through adversity? What about gaining wisdom to pass on to the next generation? What about lessons learned so as not to repeat the same mistakes?

My dad's legacy to me is a mixed bag. While he was pretty much an absentee father—business trips and late-night "appointments"—he could have impacted my young life positively. In his prime, he was a great athlete—baseball, basketball, football. "Crazy Legs Beveridge" they called him, and he operated a single-wing offense for the Butler Bulldogs during the Depression years. Several colleges offered him scholarships and he was considering taking that next step—until the final game of his senior year in high school when he took a nasty hit to his knee, ending his dream of playing college football. But without that injury, my brothers and I may never have come into this world. During World War II, many of my fathers' friends volunteered for the Armed Forces, but never returned from defeating the Nazi regime and their Allies—Italy and Japan. My father did what he could by joining the 3-C Corps (Civilian Conservation Corps).

After the war, he returned to his passion of basketball. During the war years, he had been a great basketball coach too, leading the Bulldogs to the county and state regional championships three out of four of those years. Just think what he could have taught *me*—his son! With my two older brothers already out of the nest and on their own, my dad could have been my best friend and mentor. But all I got from him were some random five-minute sessions after work when we'd shoot a few hoops or play a game of Horse before he would say, "I'm done," and sit down with the evening paper. Even then, I never heard an encouraging word from him. Never heard an "I love you, son," or "I'm proud of you!"

For all his faults as a father, Dad was an outstanding salesman, with honors and accolades bestowed by the industry. Later, I was debating what career path to take. Schoolteacher? Yeah, maybe. Farmer? Now that was more like it! But he offered me a job with his company. Although I would have preferred farming—and did that for a while after my marriage, juggling farm duties with learning Dad's business—I decided that I could enjoy helping people "grow" their net worth, both spiritually and financially.

One trait I inherited from him gave me some job satisfaction early on. I learned that, like my father, I had sales savvy. Ever try selling an invisible product? That takes the instinct to present a convincing argument to buyers in the face of providing nothing tangible to take home with them except a piece of paper. Then there was also his skill as an innovator. He introduced some tools of the trade that I capitalized on—the flip chart, for example— adding my own brand of salesmanship as I moved into wealth management. But more about that later.

In the husband and father categories, though, my dad fell far short. In fact, with my mom especially, he was a real jerk. Oh, not in her words—she would never have used that term—but in the silent language of her heart that crept into the lines of her face...

• • •

Mom was the glue that held my world together. It was Mom who read Bible stories to me every night when I was a youngster. It was Mom who took me to our little church three times a week and instilled in me the fear of God. At the age of 13, I asked Christ into my heart to be my Savior and was baptized in the creek behind our house. It was Mom who taught me a strong work ethic and encouraged me to be the best I could be. Yet all this time, I was wondering why she often looked so sad.

Oh, I knew she and Dad were not getting along. They covered their displeasure with one another in public, and no other family member suspected the trouble brewing in our household. But I felt the tension in the air and the awkward silence when relatives gathered for special occasions.

One day is indelibly carved deep in my memory. I was only sixteen. After coming home from track practice, I dropped my muddy track shoes inside the front door. After days of hearing my parents' shouting matches, the house seemed eerily quiet.

Hearing a slight noise from the basement, I ran down the stairs only to find my dad standing in front of the gun safe, shotgun in hand—and it wasn't hunting season.

"Dad! *What are you doing!?*"

He shrugged wearily. "I've had enough of her nagging and getting on my case. I've done nothing wrong. Can't take it anymore."

"But what about me?" I screamed at him, grabbing the gun from his hand. "Where's Mom?"

"Upstairs, I guess."

Racing up the stairs, two at a time, I found the bathroom door locked. Inside, I could hear her crying. "Mom! Mom, open the door!"

Slowly, she unlocked it and let me in. Her hair was a mess, her face tearstained. In her hand was a bottle of sleeping pills. It was pretty clear what she was planning to do. "I'm sorry, honey, but your dad...he doesn't really love me," she mumbled. "He has... other women in his life."

Maybe it was selfish of me at this terrible time, but I repeated what I had asked my dad. "What about me, Mom? What about *me*?"

She sighed and handed me the bottle of pills. "Don't worry, son. I won't try this again. And I won't divorce your father. I need to be here...for you."

From Mom, I gained the greatest gifts a person can inherit—faith, love, and the will to live and make something of myself, no matter the circumstances. Later, when the time was right, I would plunge into the world of wealth management, but not before I had made some *spiritual* calculations.

BEFORE YOU BUILD

With the 2020 pandemic and accompanying economic downturn that left everyone from Wall Street to your street gasping for air, the resulting social distancing and isolation gave people some unstructured time. The unexpected benefit was time to reflect, to consider what is truly worthwhile and what we wish we had done differently.

Another unfortunate incident occurred during my teen years. I had just returned from a great week at church camp—Camp Otyokwa—that I had attended every summer since sixth grade. Camp life was one of the fondest memories of my childhood, allowing me to escape from the trauma at home.

Each year, camp was a time to renew old friendships and make new ones. Once we arrived, we were assigned to a team named after the Twelve Tribes of Israel. Each team would accumulate points based on such tasks as keeping the cabin clean, taking out the trash, memorizing Bible verses, and, my personal favorite, participating in sporting events. My friend Ronnie and I competed in all of them—ping pong, softball, swimming, volleyball, and track—finishing in the top three in every sport except swimming. Both of us swam like a rock!

While at church camp, we met a couple of girls we liked and made plans to meet up with them when we got home. But little did I know that Ronnie, who attended our little church in Butler, suffered from depression, and a few days after camp, he decided to end his life. I didn't see it coming! Carrying his casket down the steps of our small country church with some of our classmates seemed surreal. That scene still haunts me to this day.

There will always be a hole in my heart over the loss of my friend. As I write this book during a pandemic, with its enforced lockdowns and accompanying isolation, the incidents of suicide have only increased. Those of us left behind are devastated. Words cannot describe the despair we feel when someone we know ends their life tragically.[1]

If you are up on your history, you will remember reading about the rash of suicides—failed banks causing some businessmen to jump out of windows and off bridges—after the crash of 1929.[3] Others, during this pandemic, have lost jobs or been furloughed

---

1 Please consider making a donation to suicideprevention@33forever.life.

with little hope of returning to their former place of employment. When some people lose all their money, they mistakenly believe all hope is gone.

But there is hope through God's Spirit and good friends to encourage us to "press on," as my brother Lyle would say. Ronnie's death did cause me to reevaluate my own life and how I might have been a better friend to him—and maybe how I could resolve the problem of my tragic home life.

• • •

For me, the number-one issue was unforgiveness. I had to wrestle with my father wound before I could succeed on any level, including my career.

Unless you get your spiritual life in order, it really doesn't matter how much money you have or how many boats, cars, real estate, or other items you possess, or even how healthy your investment portfolio might be. It doesn't matter if you are wildly successful or a big, fat failure in the world's view. What matters is whether you are meeting God's standard of success.

The answer came when I paused long enough to hear what the Lord was saying to me. The message could not have been clearer. It sounded like a divine ultimatum:

> "If you forgive men when they sin against you, your
> heavenly Father will also forgive you. But if you do not
> forgive men their sins, your Father will not forgive your
> sins."

Really, Lord? I thought. *My dad hurt me. Has never been there for me. When I was living at home, he treated me as if I didn't matter, didn't exist...* (Matthew 6:14–15)

But there it was in black and white—*forgive!* I had to admit that I was harboring resentment and bitterness toward my dad—a deadly combination—and I had to do something about it.

Forgiving my father was the first step toward freedom and, ultimately, success in every realm of my life. I can't say it was an easy process. Contributing to my depression was my junior high principal, who might have spelled further disaster in my already fragile emotional state. Calling me into his office one day, he said, "Beveridge, I've seen you strutting around the halls like you've got a chip on your shoulder. You don't perform well in the classroom, yet you've earned one of the highest IQ test scores in the class. You'd better straighten up, or you'll be in real trouble!"

What I desperately needed to hear at that moment was not condemnation but, "Hey, what's going on? How can I help?"

Instead, I heard, "If you don't fit into our box, conform to our standards, you're always going to be a loser!"

If it hadn't been for Jimmy Boyd, who came into my life about that time, I don't know where I'd be. We began spending time together, sitting on a park bench near the bandstand in downtown Bellville. We dreamed like any other 15-year-old males of that era, imagining ourselves someday as sports heroes in football or basketball and watching the pretty girls go by. When we were not fantasizing about our future, we would be shooting hoops in Jimmy's driveway or playing Horse. Even with his asthma, Jimmy was such a good friend that he would risk his health to run with me at times. Then there were the overnights at his house—anything to escape my own dismal home life and the incessant bickering between my parents.

When we graduated high school, Jimmy transferred from Ohio State to Otterbein, where I was studying for a degree in business, and became my college roommate for our last three years. Not sure I would have survived without his friendship.

• • •

I was one of those "misfits" and had to learn the hard way. In my late twenties, I began receiving therapy. But it took several face-to-face meetings with my father over the next ten years before he could admit his affairs. I do not recall that he ever asked me to forgive him for what he had put me through. He did apologize to my mother in his seventies when he had his first heart attack, but she, too, had a hard time letting the hurt go. It was not until my dad was in his eighties that the two of us could finally put away the past, and he was able to tell me he loved me and was proud of how we had grown the business. Some things just take time.

THE VALUE OF TIME

Like stocks, bonds, and other investments, time is a valuable commodity. If used wisely, it can help produce great wealth of character, as well as financial wealth. In the past, I had allowed too much time to pass, too much distance between my father and myself. Now, as I reflect on those "lost" years as they relate to in-vestment counseling, I think I am better able to offer much more than financial advice to my clients in building true net worth that outlasts time itself.

Ever since entering the business world, it has been my desire to establish a long-term relationship with every one of my cli-ents—not just as a hit-and-run financial advisor. So, thanks for listening to a bit of my story. If we were working together, I would want to know *yours* too. By now, however, you may be wondering what all of that has to do with building your net worth.

Maybe the explanation is in the definition of *net worth*. This term can be defined as "a measure of wealth. The sum of all assets owned by a person or company, minus any obligations or liabil-ities."[4] In short, net worth is what you have left if you were to sell all you owned—house, property, cars, jewelry, etc.—and paid off all your debts.

But there is a deeper definition of this phrase in my opinion. True net worth is not the product of some financial formula. It is not the accumulation of stuff. It is not even the balance you achieve when you subtract your bad deeds from your good deeds. True net worth is accepting yourself for who God created you to be and using your talents and abilities to reach your full potential.

When I took over the helm of E.S. Beveridge and Associates, Inc. (ESB) when my dad retired, I still had much to learn, which I now intend to pass on to you, my readers.

HOW TO PICK A WINNER
(When Shopping for a Financial Advisor)

As a financial professional, one of the first things I attempted was to make sure that our company was worthy of our clients' trust. For example, who would consult an unlicensed physician for advice on some illness or medical emergency? Advisors like myself are licensed with FINRA® (Financial Industry Regulatory Authority), the SEC (Securities and Exchange Commission), Life and Health Insurance licenses for the state in which you reside, and AIF® (Accredited Investment Fiduciary). We carry those licenses and designations to assure our clients that we are thoroughly trained and backed by a third-party auditor who oversees our operation.

In scouting out someone to help build your financial plan, look for an advisor who is licensed, independent, and has a great track record. You can also do your research under FINRA broker check or any state insurance department website. Always ask for references. It's easy to give financial advice over a radio or TV show because that person usually assumes no fiduciary responsibility once the show is over or the caller hangs up. So, beware of accepting advice from someone you will never see again after the initial visit or viewing. In other words, no follow-up. I'm not saying that all such advice is bad. I just want to caution you to do your research before you follow blindly.

I believe in developing client relationships for the long haul. Many of my clients live in my community, so I see them at sporting events, the hardware store, the grocery, and church. By knowing their lifestyle and their habits, I am better able to advise them and look out for their interests.

In our company, with prospective clients who desire our services, we start out by suggesting five strategies, which we call our 5D Process:

1. *Discover*—At ESB, we want you to get to know us, our culture, our services, and how we can help you reach your investment and retirement goals.

2. *Disclose*—*You* are our most important asset! We want to get to know *you,* your lifestyle, your unique identity, your dreams and aspirations, your financial needs and goals. Much like your doctor, who needs certain information in order to diagnose a medical problem, we need to collect data that will give us an accurate picture of your personal life. Therefore, we want to listen!

3. *Develop*—Once we have a clear understanding of you and your potential financial future—and if you feel that we are a good fit—it is time to formulate a customized plan together. With mutual trust established, we are ready to discuss how and in what to invest.

4. *Destiny*—Upon your death, how do we facilitate the distribution of your hard-earned assets? Will your beneficiaries be your children, grandchildren, church, or other institutions?

5. *Divest*—The execution of number 4, which takes place after you pass away. But don't be too hasty! As the old sayings go, "You don't want to get undressed until you're ready to go to bed" or "sell the farm until you're through farming!"

SO...WHAT ABOUT THE "LONG RUN"?

As I write these words, recalling a lifetime invested in helping others with their financial needs, I am struck with the parallels between accumulating and managing material wealth and doing the same regarding spiritual wealth. Interestingly, our company guidelines for advisor-client relations mirror our relationship with God.

Not only is the wealth of heaven far greater than any that can be accumulated on earth, but it cannot be stolen, forged, embezzled, or lost. Therefore, it seems wise to calculate how we might be best storing up eternal treasures during our short time here.

1. *Discover*—your true net worth in God. The formula is different from that used in the earthly realm. Remember, our net worth is not good deeds minus bad deeds. For believers, our worth is measured by what our Creator feels about us:

> All of you are children of the Most High.
> (Psalm 82:6, see also John 3:16; 1 Peter 2:9.)

2. *Disclose*—your daily need of His provision and grace. Be honest! He already knows anyway, so don't be afraid to confess your weaknesses and temptations and let Him reveal strategies for overcoming them.

> Have mercy on me, O God....
> Wash away all my iniquity,

and cleanse me from my sin.
For I know my transgressions,
and my sin is always before me.
(Psalm 51:1–3, see also Psalm 6:1, 2; Romans 3:23.)

3. *Develop*—"Grow" spiritual wealth through talking with God and listening to His answers, reading His Word, obeying His commandments, developing intimacy with Him, and loving and caring for others.

In everything by prayer and petition,
with thanksgiving, present your requests to God.
And the peace of God, which transcends all under-
standing, will guard your hearts and your minds in
Christ Jesus.
(Philippians 4:6, see also Psalm 119:16;
Deuteronomy 4:30–31.)

4. *Destiny*—If you are a believer, heaven and all its glory await you. Learn to be heavenly minded, not earth-bound. We are not citizens of this world, but of the one to come. So store up heavenly treasures.

Praise be to the God and Father of our Lord Jesus
Christ!
In his great mercy he has given us new birth into a
living hope through the resurrection of Jesus Christ
from the dead, and into an inheritance that can never
perish, spoil, or fade—kept in heaven for you.
(1 Peter 1:3–4, see also Psalm 16:11; 2 Timothy 4:8; Revelation 21:4.)

5. *Divest*—When your days on earth are over, consider now what your legacy will be. How will you be remembered? What have you invested in others that will continue to live on?

> A good man leaves an inheritance to his children's children, but a sinner's wealth is stored up for the righteous. (Proverbs 13:22, see also Proverbs 10: 4–5; Ephesians 1:18.)

In his book, *Quiet Strength,* the great football coach of the Tampa Bay Buccaneers and the Indianapolis Colts, Tony Dungy, said, "We are all role models, and we all can and should have a positive impact on someone's life. God has placed each of us where we are for a reason: within our spheres of influence at work, in our neighborhoods, in our families. He wants us to touch lives wherever He leads us.

"Whether you are a friend to a bullied boy in middle school, a ray of light in your neighborhood book club, a supportive coach for a high school team, an available shoulder to someone at a time of loss, or a handheld out to a child looking for a little hope, we all can change the course of our nation and world, one life at a time, for the rest of our lives."[5]

We are living in unprecedented times. It is a time to remember our purpose. It is a time to forget past sins, insults, and injuries—if they have been forgiven and resolved. It is a time to reassess and a time to reset. As long as we have breath in our bodies, there is time to prepare for the financial and spiritual legacy we will leave behind.

> Bottom Line: *No matter your age, if you are still holding onto bitterness, hurt, and unforgiveness toward someone, how will you ever build true net worth? So, take some time out to consider what is truly important. It's your life! It's your money! It's your opportunity!*

Chapter 2

THE MULTIPLICATION FACTOR

God blessed them [the first man and woman], And said
to them, "Be fruitful and increase in number [multiply];
fill the earth and subdue it. (Genesis 1:28)

MY WIFE, KIM, and I were married on August 5, 1978, the same
day my mom and dad had tied the knot forty years earlier. A little
over a year later, our first child, Aaron, was born. Now, working
in my father's insurance firm and at home, the multiplication
factor was in full swing. In the next four years, I did my best to
learn the insurance business, and my wife and I added two more
children to our family.

Nothing in my Otterbein University history and education
classes (after switching from a degree in Business), had prepared me for selling life and health insurance. I wasn't even sure
I wanted to be a salesman. When I graduated, I had thought I
was headed for a career as a schoolteacher. But after a disastrous
student teaching experience, I realized I did not fit the culture
that permeated our educational system. I much preferred farm

life—the peaceful out-of-doors where I could see things grow right before my eyes rather than waiting out the long-term results of investing in kids or clients. Still, I failed to launch my chosen profession. Strike one!

My second failure came several years later. While saving money to purchase our first home, Kim and I were renting a small place near my parents' farm. I was trying to learn the insurance business during office hours, then rushing back to work the farm, logging a total of ten to twelve hours a day. This is when I discovered that I wasn't cut out for farming either. Since I am not mechanically inclined, I was unable to repair farm equipment when it broke down. I was also fast learning that even two hundred acres was insufficient to support our growing family.

With two strikes against me, I was somewhat prepared for Kim's reaction one night when I came in from the barn, where I had worked hard to save several sick lambs—and failed. Slumping into a chair in our family room, I buried my head in my hands. "And that isn't all," I confessed. "I couldn't fix the manure spreader today."

She sighed and gave it to me straight. "You know you can't keep working like this, Kyle. You're going to have to choose."

It was a tough decision. As much as I loved the farm, I was going to have to fully commit to a business that would provide for my family. That business involved selling, using the power of persuasion.

And herein lies another failure from my past. Stuttering.

One of the most frightening experiences for the majority of people—"a fear greater than death," according to several professional surveys—is the idea of standing in front of a group and giving a speech. I was in that majority as a teenager.

In fact, in FFA (Future Farmers of America), I had no clue that part of the requirement was to give at least two speeches before the class each semester. Even when my guidance counselor suggested that speech class might help, my stuttering did not improve, and this impediment persisted throughout my high school years.

It was not until my first semester at Otterbein University that a professor picked up on my problem and offered a solution to the first speech I would give in his class. After pulling me aside to talk with me, he said, "You don't have a speech problem. You have a confidence problem. Just talk about something you're good at—like cross country." I did, and in giving that speech, I didn't stutter once!

But selling life insurance was not something that I was overly familiar with, and the ghost of failures past came back to haunt me. How could I sell something new to me without stumbling over my words—and losing a potential client? The possibility always loomed over me like a dark cloud.

By now, of course, I had associated this "failure" with my troubled childhood—particularly my father's lack of love and attention. Ironically, *he* was the one I would have to depend upon to mentor me in the process of learning the business.

RICH MAN, POOR MAN

My father was the quintessential "rich man, poor man"—rich in this world's goods and currency maybe, but poor in the things that really matter. Despite our differences, as I have mentioned, he was a great salesman and a member of the Million Dollar Round Table—a noteworthy achievement for a high school graduate with no formal training. To earn that prestigious award, one must sell a million dollars of life insurance, death benefits, and whole life insurance every year for ten successive years. One thing for sure—I was learning from the best.

You also know that my dad was an innovator. As a believer in the old saying, "A picture is worth a thousand words," he was one of the first to use a flip chart to illustrate the benefits of life insurance. The first time he used his flip chart when making a presentation to the local Life Underwriters meeting, he received a standing ovation. I made good use of that idea, embellishing it through the years with some additions of my own.

I am especially grateful that he taught me the value of incentives. With no incentive to perform on the job any better than the next person, you will never achieve your greatest potential. In most cases, American workers are given incentives—higher pay, promotion, job satisfaction. My father taught me to take ownership of every sales pitch. To develop a sense of pride in my work. To reach higher. To go for the gold!

A bit later in this chapter, I will share with you how we built our business to twenty times its worth since I joined the family firm in 1978. But there is really nothing new here. The principles date back to biblical times. See if you can find the business model by connecting the dots in the following stories.

JACOB AND HIS "BAD BOSS"
(Genesis 29–31, author paraphrase)

A favorite role model in terms of outstanding work ethic—even after his failures in other ways—is Jacob. The meaning of his name, "deceiver," gives us an idea of the man's character in his youth. In a brazen act of deception, Jacob convinced his dying father to give *him* the family blessing rather than Esau, his older brother and the rightful heir.

Escaping Esau's outrage over losing his birthright, Jacob fled to the home of their father's brother, Laban. There he quickly spotted Laban's beautiful younger daughter, Rachel, and was smitten at first glance. *That's the girl for me,* he thought. *I must have her for my wife—whatever it takes.*

And this reminds me of that sultry summer night at the Bellville ball field. I was leaning over the fence watching the game when I spotted her in the stands. She was eyeing me too, as she tossed her long, dark hair over her shoulders. I would be off to college in the fall while she was still in high school. Yet I knew then that she was the girl for me...and I would wait for her...however long it took.

What it "took" for Jacob was seven years of hard labor, tending his uncle's flocks and herds! Jacob got a taste of his own medicine at the hands of his Uncle Laban, who was not only a calculating boss but also his future father-in-law.

At the end of the seven years, the wedding day finally arrived. The bride, heavily veiled in the custom of that day, was presented to Jacob. *At last!* he thought to himself. *I am finally receiving the reward for my diligence.* Only on the wedding night did he discover his new wife's true identity. It was not Rachel—his beloved—but her older sister Leah.

Unwilling to lose the woman he loved, Jacob agreed to another seven-year contract with his conniving uncle. During those fourteen years, Jacob was tricked multiple times with ten changes in wages and other unfair practices. But he persevered. Meanwhile, with two wives now, his family grew as children were born to both Rachel and Leah.

But that's not the end of the tale. There was yet another disappointing turn of events when Jacob was forced to work six more years for flocks and herds of his own before he could leave with his large family. During that time, God downloaded the secret to accumulating those flocks and herds and Jacob left a wealthy man, having learned lessons of creativity and innovation in business that would stand him in good stead in future years.

On the return to his homeland, a dramatic, face-to-face encounter with God changed his life—and his name—forever. *"Your name shall no longer be called Jacob, but Israel [Prince of God],"* said the Lord. Later came this amazing promise: *"I am God Almighty. Be fruitful and increase in number. A nation and a community of nations will come from you, and kings will come from your body"* (Genesis 35:11).

Talk about a success story. From selfish, grasping deceiver to prince of God and father of nations! God's multiplied blessings.

ELIJAH AND A WIDOW'S LAST MEAL
(1 Kings 17:8–16, author paraphrase)

An example of prophetic vision and obedience is the prophet Elijah. During a great drought, God spoke to him, instructing him to travel to a certain city where he would find a widow and her son. He was to stay with them where God Himself would provide for them.

Can you imagine the level of faith that journey must have required? Elijah might have questioned whether he was hearing correctly during a global crisis. And what might a woman in those days have felt if a strange man invited himself into her home? Wouldn't she have been suspicious of his motives? Frightened for herself and her child? Besides, what would the neighbors think? Not to mention that, under normal circumstances, any good homemaker would have wanted to offer a guest the best in food and hospitality.

In the village of Zarephath, Elijah met the woman and, sure enough, the first thing he did was to ask her for a little bread and water.

Since there had been no rain for quite some time, the crops had withered on the vine, and the food was all but gone. "I'm sorry, sir," she said, "but there is scarcely a morsel in the house. Nothing but a handful of flour and a little oil in a jar. I was going to make a small meal for my son and myself before we die of starvation."

Following the divine instructions he had received, Elijah said, "Don't be afraid to do what I ask. Just make something for me first, then for the two of you. The Lord has promised me that you will have plenty of flour and oil to last until the rain comes to break the drought. You will not lack for food during this famine."

Plenty! You will not lack! God has promised!

Miracles still happen—sometimes right in front of you. You simply must take the leap of faith and trust God. You need to take what you have and multiply it—whether moving your family to another state, applying for a new job, or deciding when and where to invest your money. If you don't change your way of thinking or your attitude in leveraging your God-given opportunities, you're probably going to find yourself stuck in the cycle of poverty with nothing but "a handful of flour." Sometimes you just have to trust God to turn your "nothing" into "plenty."

JESUS AND A LITTLE BOY'S LUNCH
(John 6:1–14, author paraphrase)

Crowds often gathered to hear the revolutionary Teacher from Galilee. This time, it was a "multitude" of five thousand men, not counting women and children. Among the younger people was a little boy, eager to hear the "Man on the Mountain" he had heard so much about. He had brought a lunch (his mom had probably packed it for him)—five barley loaves and two small fish.

When the afternoon wore on and the people were hungry, Jesus was moved with compassion and asked His disciples where they might buy food. "Master," replied one of them, "it would cost a fortune to feed this crowd!"

Andrew had spotted the boy with the lunch and mentioned it to Jesus with a sigh. "But what good would that do, Master, when there are so many?"

Just watch what happened next. You know the story. Jesus took that small lunch, blessed it, and when the disciples distributed the food, there was more than enough to go around, with twelve baskets of leftovers!

What do you have in your hand? On your mind? In your bank account? Take whatever you have—no matter how meager—offer it to God, and watch Him multiply it. His strategies are guaranteed to work, and the returns are eternal. And never discount the young ones. God often gives them wisdom beyond their years.

RAY KROC—"MR. BIG MAC"

As I mentioned in the introduction to this book, there are over two thousand references to wealth and money in the Bible. We have just read about three of them. But I am also inspired to hear the stories of some of our contemporaries who have learned how God's principle of multiplication can lead to success in our time. Meet Ray Kroc, former milkshake mixer salesman who was later named as one of *Time* magazine's "Most Important People of the Century." It was Ray who expanded McDonald's brand to worldwide status as "the most famous and successful fast-food restaurant in the world."[6]

Buying out the founders in 1961, Ray quickly multiplied the little hamburger joint he had discovered in San Bernardino, California, to seven hundred franchises across the country. His strategy was to sell to local operators, insisting on standardized procedures for food preparation and packaging. In addition, he developed a training program for new, young employees to learn the trade, insisting on quality, service, cleanliness, and value.

By 2003, McDonald's had gone global, serving millions in 119 countries and pulling in $17 billion. McDonald's mission statement reflects many of our own core values at ESB:

- We place customer experience at the core of all we do.
- We are committed to our people.
- We operate our business ethically.
- We grow our business profitably.
- We strive continually to improve.
- We give back to our communities.

"Acknowledging the importance of the needs and preferences of the customers is highly valued at McDonald's. The company also encourages respect for people, the brand of the company and a call to always operate in a justified manner. By weaving the needs of the communities with those of the business, McDonald's has created an environment where all partners thrive."[7]

Ray Kroc was an entrepreneur who loved God, family, and McDonald's—although not necessarily in that order! He died a fabulously wealthy man with a company net worth of $8 billion and a personal net worth of $600 million.[8] In distributing his wealth to worthy individuals and institutions, his widow, Joan Kroc, became known as one of the twentieth century's greatest philanthropists. *He* made the money and, after his death, *she* gave it all away!

FROM CRACK ADDICT TO CEO

You know Mike. *Everyone* knows Mike. Even the 45th President of the United States said, "That guy has been on television more than anyone I know, including *me!*" If you watch much TV, you've surely seen Mike Lindell on countless commercial breaks, pitching his famous pillows and mattress toppers and guaranteeing that "you'll have the best sleep of your entire life!"

But Mike hasn't always been a successful entrepreneur. In his book *What Are the Odds?*, he tells the story of his transformation from crack addict to CEO. Today, after a string of failures and life-altering poor decisions, he heads one of the fastest-growing companies in America. Proof that, with prayer and perseverance, anyone can achieve his or her purpose in life.

Dr. Ben Carson, pediatric neurosurgeon and a member of President Trump's administration, had this to say about Mike and his phenomenal success against all odds: "MyPillow is the most successful direct marketing product in the history of America.... You don't have to know its inventor very long to see why. Mike Lindell is a natural marketer.... God gives everyone special gifts, but He also places challenges in our way to make us stronger. Some people meet these challenges head-on right away, inspiring us all. Others take a 'broken road,' overcoming not only external challenges, but perhaps the greatest obstacle of all—themselves."[9]

I may not have been afflicted with the moral weaknesses that plagued Mike—drug addiction, alcoholism, gambling—but I have had my fair share of struggles and failures. I, too, found myself on a "broken road."

Very few of my friends knew of my disastrous family life because I covered up my insecurities with a cocky attitude. And then...adolescence set in. It seemed that every day I would wake up, look in the mirror, and discover another big zit on my face. To compound my misery, that's when I started stuttering. Couldn't speak more than a sentence or two without fumbling for words. Not a promising profile for a sophomore in high school.

In desperation, one of my outlets became track and cross country. When I would find my mother and dad at each other's throats, I'd go for a long run—six miles from our house in town to the farm—then turn around and run home again.

At my mother's insistence, I also learned the value of hard work. The summer I was sixteen, she suggested I take on a project funded by the federal government. If a landowner didn't farm certain hilly land, the government would pay x number of dollars, which I could keep if I cleared the land. *Count me in!* I thought. We had an old Ford tractor and a brush-hog mower, and it took me all summer to mow those seventy acres. But that became another outlet for my increasing anger and anxiety.

Over a period of time, I saved $1,500—enough to buy myself a souped-up motorcycle, which I would ride to escape the tensions that continually flared in our household. Probably not the best decision for a frustrated teenager who could gun the engine from 0 to 60 miles per hour in four seconds. Like Mike, God's hand was on my life!

Now, Lindell, with a net worth of $300 million, uses his platform to share not only his wealth, but his testimony of what God has done for him. Many of his employees in the pillow factory are recovering addicts. What God has done for Mike, He can do for them—and millions of others!

"WEALTH: IS IT WORTH IT?"

Truett Cathy, a businessman who was called "one of the most generous people in the world," was the founder of the famous Chick-fil-A restaurant chain, which currently has over 1,500 restaurants in 39 states. But that's not all. Truett also operated 12 foster homes, started a summer camp for children, and has handed out more than $26 million in scholarships to team members working for him. For over sixty years he taught a boys' Sunday school class and created a foundation that will continue to touch young lives for future generations.

As a billionaire, Mr. Cathy has observed the power of wealth to both bless and curse. Two of his wealthy friends ended up in divorce, having lost their businesses, and a third is facing bankruptcy through misuse of money, leading Truett to question:

"Wealth: Is It Worth It?"—the title of his autobiography.[10] Personally, he has always taken the high ground, giving away much of his own money and teaching others to treasure the most important things in life—faith, hope, and love.

Such a man inspires me to "go and do likewise."

• • •

Today I realize that I am blessed with a great family and great business associates. Even with all the chaos caused by the pandemic and the highs and lows of the financial industry, our business continues to thrive. And I have had to ask myself why, when others are going under.

Like Jacob, I have had to overcome family dysfunction as well as my own personality flaws and failures—but Jacob and I didn't give up. *"Can't* died in the poorhouse," as my mother used to say. Instead, we sought God for a blessing. As a result, He changed Jacob's name and his nature and caused him to prosper just as I have through these years.

Like Elijah, just when everything seems bleak and barren and the stock market dips, I can count on God to direct me to the next phase of our work and multiply our assets as he multiplied the grain and oil for the widow of Zarephath.

Like a little boy's lunch, I can give to Jesus whatever is in my "hand"—my dad's business savvy, my mom's love, devotion, and spiritual nurturing, along with all that I have learned. In *His* hands, my clients, my concepts, and my understanding of the times are multiplied, and He takes me to the next level.

Bottom Line: *The greatest asset in any business is people— your staff, your associates, your clients. These are the multipliers that will ensure growth and help you increase the value of your enterprise.*

Chapter 3

THE POWER OF EQUITY INVESTING

"History convincingly demonstrates that stocks have been and will remain the best investment for all those seeking long-term gains."
–Jeremy J. Siegel, *Stocks for the Long Run*

"TOO RISKY! I can't afford to lose money in the stock market!"

"I thought investing was only for rich people."

"I've heard a lot recently about investing in gold. Maybe that's where I ought to put my money."

"Huh! Might as well be gambling in Las Vegas. Isn't that about the same as making an investment in the stock market these days?"

And then there are those who procrastinate. As my mother often quoted, "Never put off until tomorrow what you can do today!"

As a financial advisor and business owner for forty-plus years, I have heard these and plenty of other excuses for hesitating, staunchly refusing to invest in the stock market, or even considering developing a financial plan. Therefore, my intent in this chapter is to put to rest the myths, misunderstandings, and outright misrepresentations of the truth of investing in stocks on the path to building your net worth.

DEMYSTIFYING THE MYTHS:
MYTH #1: TOO RISKY.

Yes—if you invest for only a short period of time. We like to encourage investors to leave their money with us for at least five years. That gives us time to strategize and explore the stocks, or equities, that are best for you. If you think certain stocks are too risky, that is because you have a short-term approach to investing.

But deciding that you're not going to invest in the stock market because your grandparents lost a fortune in the Great Depression of 1929 is like LeBron James—who is 6'8", can run like a gazelle, and can shoot a basket from the three-point line—saying, "Well, think I'll sit this one out. I've watched my buddies miss too many shots. I just might miss one too." Winners get in the game and give it their best; they don't stand idly by on the sidelines and worry about missing a shot.

Actually, risk is a part of life. The only way to avoid it is to distance yourself permanently from anyone or anything that could possibly cause you harm. That means: No more picnics—what if you were stung by a wasp or a horsefly? No close friends—what if one of them betrayed your friendship? And absolutely no investing—what if the pandemic turned out to recur again and again and crushed the economy with what appeared to be no hope of recovery?

We can't live by the what-ifs of life. Undoubtedly, we have experienced an unprecedented global crisis, but this is not the time to retreat. Interestingly, "the word crisis in Chinese is composed of two characters: the first, the symbol of danger...the second, of opportunity."[11] Which will it be for you? Will you run away from the danger, the uncertainty...or seize the opportunity?

MYTH #2: INVESTING IS ONLY FOR RICH FOLKS.

Wrong! If you can come up with an extra $50 a month, you can begin investing in a good mutual fund. (See Chart 1 at the back of this book.) That's all it would take to build a comfortable retirement fund or nest egg for easy accessibility during hard times, and this small amount is affordable for most people. If not, you might need to make a simple lifestyle change—like not eating out several times a month or giving up desserts that only add pounds and increase your waistline, not your bottom line. Keep reading for tips on how, where, and when to invest in stocks.

For example, in the following chapter, you will learn how a newlywed couple on a limited income applied common sense, discipline, and hard work to that small amount of money each month to build their net worth. You can do that too. This couple didn't wait to pay off all their debt to begin investing. They just began investing at the beginning of their marriage—and it has already paid off!

MYTH #3: INVEST IN GOLD: IT WILL ALWAYS HOLD ITS VALUE.

True to a point. But have you ever tried buying your groceries at Kroger or shopping at Walmart with gold coins? Awkward for the cashier making change, to say the least. There is nothing wrong with owning some gold, but it is best not to make it more than 10% to 20% of your total investment since gold pays no interest or dividends.

That has not always been the case. In the book of Matthew, Jesus tells the story of a wealthy landowner who decided to test three of his most trusted managers by giving each of them some bags of gold. To the one with the most experience, he gave five bags of gold. To the one with slightly less experience, he gave two bags. To the least experienced manager, he gave only one bag.

The businessman then left for a trip to check on some of his other ventures. Upon his return several months later, he called a meeting of the managers to report on their earnings. The first manager was pleased to report that he had doubled his investment. The second was equally productive, increasing his two bags of gold to four.

But the third manager said to his boss, "Lord, I knew that you are a hard man....So I was afraid and went out and hid your talent [gold] in the ground. See, here is what belongs to you" (Matthew 25:24–25).

Instead of being proud of his employee for not losing any of the gold, the landowner was irate. "You wicked, lazy servant! ... You should have put my money on deposit with the bankers, so that when I returned I would have received it back with interest" (v. 26).

So...what happened here? The key word in the third manager's explanation is afraid. Fear is a debilitating problem that affects too many. Fear causes some to become hooked on opioids. Fear robs others of realizing their dreams—marriage or having children or starting a business or...investing in the stock market!

The odd thing about this story is that the wealthy landowner took the bag of gold from the ineffective manager and gave it to the one who had invested wisely. But remember: With an increase in net worth comes also an increase in responsibility. Now this man has the opportunity to re-invest or to share his wealth with the needy. No other system provides this kind of freedom.

The government should not be the source nor the instrument of promoting economic equality.

MYTH #4: INVESTING IS A GAME OF CHANCE.

This is no game. It is a sound and sensible approach to building a financial safety net that will see you through the ups and downs of this life. (Refer to Chart 1 at the back of this book.)

If you are a gambler, unless you have a photographic memory, you never know what card is going to be flipped next or whether you will have four of a kind. Blackjack, poker, you name it—they are just games. On the other hand, if you do your homework and know something about the stock market or engage a good financial team, you will know that when you invest in the market, you become a stockholder. You are actually buying a small percentage of a company or companies. With a minimal outlay of money, you become an owner! Therefore, you will gain a return on your investment as the company (or companies) prosper. You may also hit a downturn occasionally. But if you hold that "hand" for the long haul, you stand to come out ahead.

To help you make decisions as to ownership of stock, the majority of the time we suggest that you "buy what you buy." In other words, think of those necessities of life—electricity, water, gas, food, healthcare, technology—and, knowing they aren't going away any time soon, you can feel safe in investing in those companies. On a humorous note, one of the best stocks to own during the pandemic was Smucker's, the jelly company. A few years ago, they bought Jif, the peanut butter brand, from Procter & Gamble. Therefore, during a hurricane or a pandemic lockdown, there is always the makings of a good PB&J sandwich in the pantry!

Before you buy, though, I recommend that you read the following books to give you a feel for the market:

- *Stocks for the Long Run* by Jeremy Siegel
- *The Total Money Makeover* by Dave Ramsey
- *Unstoppable Prosperity* by Charles Payne

These are reputable experts in the field with much experience behind them. Still, it is always wise to sit down with the "team" I mentioned earlier. A certified financial advisor will be able to save you a lot of time and money as you draw up the plan tailored to your needs.

INVEST IN THE MARKET—IF YOU'RE NOT IN A HURRY

Dr. Jeremy Siegel said it first, but his statement bears repeating: "History convincingly demonstrates that stocks have been and will remain the best investment for all those seeking long-term gains."[12] Did you get that? Long-term gains.

It is the premise of the fable, The Tortoise and the Hare. In a race with a rabbit, known for its speed, the turtle plodded along in his turtle-like pace. The rabbit, now far ahead, decided to take a nap until the turtle caught up. Still asleep, the rabbit failed to see his opponent's approach and missed his opportunity to win the race. Yes, the turtle was slow but steady. That's a winning approach to investing too.

You have probably read about the three most widely utilized vehicles for savings—the 401(k), the traditional IRA, and the Roth IRA. But there are others with slight variations.

As for investing in stocks within these vehicles, there are at least five good reasons why I believe Dr. Siegel is right:

PERFORMANCE

Dating back to 1802, stocks have historically outperformed gold, silver, bonds, and even real estate. Once, while watching a TV business show in which the host was interviewing economist Ben Stein, I heard Mr. Stein say, "I have never seen a stock equity that needed a new roof!" If you invest in stocks, you're an owner; if you invest in bonds, you're a loaner.

PERCENTAGE

With a small amount of money—as little as that iconic $50 per month—you can begin to acquire a large portfolio of assets by investing in stocks. (Refer to Chart 1 at the back of this book.) In contrast, could you purchase a rental property for $50 per month? Or an ounce of gold, which at the time of this publication was selling for $1,900 per ounce? Or ten houses? Or shares in multiple corporations, including the giant tech companies?

POSITION
(liquidity)

Stocks, unlike other equities, are known for their liquidity. In a matter of four business days, stocks can be sold and the monies can be transferred into your bank account. For that matter, at ESB, we always recommend that our clients keep enough money in their FDIC-insured bank account so they can sleep well at night. This emergency fund guarantees that money is readily available when needed without being forced to sell stocks from your portfolio when they are at a low point.

PATIENCE

Investing in stocks is not for the faint of heart, nor the hasty. You can expect ups and downs in the value of your portfolio; there are times when you simply have to wait it out to see a return. Every eight to ten years, the stock market, as measured by the S&P

500 (a market index of the top 500 corporations, which has been around since 1956), has decreased in value by 20% or more. This downturn can result from several different factors—government missteps, government regulations, oil shocks, recessions, etc. During the '20s, many people invested in the stock market via a margin account, meaning they borrowed money against their holdings (back then, it was probably the family farm). Although today you can borrow up to 50% of the value of your holdings in your investment account, I wouldn't recommend it. Still, not a good idea.

POWER OF DIVIDENDS

The richest man in the world, John D. Rockefeller, once said, "The only thing that gives me pleasure [is] to see my dividends coming in."[3]

A dividend is the cash regularly paid to stockholders from a company's earnings, generated from products or services provided by the company. The ability to pay a consistent dividend is an indicator of that company's financial health. As I said earlier in this chapter, if you are going to purchase individual stocks, look first to companies that provide a need. Then look for companies that pay a dividend. A dividend from a company you own is like interest earned on your bank account.

Dividends are an important way to help build your net worth. Take, for example, today's CDs and money markets, yielding less than 0.6%. Even ten-year treasury bonds have fluctuated between 0.6% to 1.5% over the last year. I remember several economists predicting during the 1980s that we would never see single-digit interest rates again, yet we have been experiencing these low interest rates for some time. Good for borrowers. Bad for lenders and savers. However, as pointed out in number 3 above on liquidity, you need to be disciplined to keep at least 20% of your net worth in savings/checking/money market accounts even when they are making so little interest. This is hard to do!

Another reason dividends are important in building your net worth is explained by looking at the recent history of the S&P 500 from 1969–1981. (See Chart 2 at the back of this book.) The average dividend yield, or the dividend expressed as a percentage of the stock price, was 1.87% during that bear market when stock prices were falling and earnings declining. This decline in stock prices could be based on many factors, including the government raising interest rates to curb inflation, as in what happened from 1969–1981. For example, interest on my first mortgage was 13.5% in 1981, with my mortgage payment right at 95% in interest. Thank God, I only paid $13,000 for the house!

With double-digit interest rates on money market accounts, savings accounts, and CDs, it was difficult to consider investing in the stock market during the '70s and early '80s. But if you had bitten the bullet and invested during those years, then reinvested your dividends, you would have been handsomely rewarded from 1986–2000. Remember, a $1,000 investment in Microsoft IPO (initial public offering) in 1986 is worth over $1 million today. That could have been you! Or if you were alive in 1970 and bought 100 shares of Walmart at its IPO for $1,650 ($16.50 per share), it would be worth over $4.3 million today. So, if you work for a publicly held company and they offer you stock offerings, take them.

While we are having this discussion, may I underscore these red flags when it comes to investing?

- Never borrow money to invest in the stock market. Use extra cash.
- Never buy stocks on margin (or borrowing against the value of your stocks to buy more stocks).
- Never invest 100% of your money—at any time—because

you always need to have money to buy if the market is on sale, or something may happen that requires you to use all of your emergency fund and you need funds available.

WHAT TO DO WHEN THE MARKET IS DOWN

On the positive side, when the market is down is not the time to panic. It's the time to shop! When people go shopping, most are looking for a four-letter word: SALE!

For example, you go to the grocery store to pick up some milk with only $2.00 in your pocket. The price of milk per gallon is usually around $2.00, but you see a sign that reads: "Buy One, Get One Free!" Your $2.00 just bought you two gallons of milk instead of one. Or you walk into a shoe store, looking for some sneakers. You also need a pair of high-heeled shoes to wear to your daughter's wedding. But you have only $50 to spend, and the dress shoes cost that much. Then you notice that there is a "2 for 1 Sale" going on, so you can buy both the pumps and the running shoes, which will enable you to fit into that size-6 dress you are planning to wear to the wedding!

In other words, the stock market is a market that scouts out opportunities. And when I look for opportunities for my customers, I don't look for individual stocks. I look for sectors. For example, if I think that full-service restaurants will make a big comeback as Covid declines, I can buy this sector of the economy, which consists of dozens of good companies (using ETFs which will be explained in detail later). This is a lot less risky than trying to pick which individual restaurant stock will do well when I don't personally know the owner, CFO, CEO, or production manager.

I would be putting my money—actually, your money—at risk if I invested in a product or business where I didn't know the persons involved. It would be like buying shoes without trying them on! There is a much greater likelihood that a portfolio of restaurant stocks will do well than just picking one restaurant stock and hoping I picked the right one. It is always possible that if we try to pick just one, we could be right about the sector doing well, but end up with the one company that didn't!

THE LAW OF SUPPLY AND DEMAND

Now for a mini-refresher course. One of the basic principles of a capitalistic society is the law of supply and demand. Much has been written about it throughout the ages. In my basic macro-economics class in college, I remember my professor, Dr. Koo, engraining this philosophy into his students' brains: the greater the demand for any product or service, the higher the price can be for that product or service. The opposite is also true: too much product or service without much demand lowers the price of that product or service. The evidence today as I'm writing this book is found in the price of lumber. The demand for home project materials during the pandemic skyrocketed. But yet lumber yards were shut down for months, which led to decrease supply. So lumber prices went up about 250% because demand outstripped supply.

If you or your financial advisor buy individual stocks and the trading volume is significantly lower than its competitors in the same sector, you need to be careful. This is called "thinly traded stock" because there is low demand for that stock. Remember what I said earlier: The stock market is a lot like an auction. If only a few investors want to buy the stock you are considering buying, you may have a hard time selling it.

As I am writing this book, the NASDAQ, which is heavily loaded with tech stock, is hitting record highs. The reason is that the demand for those stocks has been increasing. The lockdown of many brick and mortar stores during the pandemic influenced many to turn to online shopping. Others are working via computer from home. A relatively new company, Zoom, which allows you to hold virtual meetings from home anywhere around the globe, is one that is "zooming" to the top. Another company that has risen dramatically for other reasons is Tesla, which has gone up nearly 1,100% since April of 2020, making a profit for the first time that year, vs. the price of GM and Ford, which was flat. Interestingly, Tesla made a profit for the first time that year. As demand for a stock increases, we see that it puts upward pressure on its price. However, don't get caught up in following the crowd, which can arbitrarily drive stock prices exorbitantly high.

You can pay way too much for a stock that is a momentum stock. In other words, you need to pay attention to the price/earnings and valuation. It's not much different from buying an antique that cost you ten times more than it is really worth because you got caught up in the momentum of an auction. Emotions often affect our decisions. Don't overpay. A good advisor will help you assess the value of a stock and caution you about paying more than it is worth. But if you have some extra money and don't mind taking a risk, go for it!

"IF ONLY..."

In the realm of finance, there are plenty of if-onlys. For example, think how much you would be worth today if only you had invested $1,000 on the day of Microsoft's IPO in March of 1983—more than $1.6 million! Of course, there is no guarantee that any new company will be successful. But who knew that Microsoft would lead the tech industry with their computers, software, and video games, or that one of its founders, Bill Gates, would become one of the youngest billionaires in the world at age 31?

If ever there was someone with a reason to defer investing in the stock market until a more convenient season, it would be me during a particularly stressful time. It was during the years when all four of our kids were in college, and our two daughters decided to get married, meaning that guess-who gets to pay for the weddings. You got it! The father of the brides! Add to that challenge the fact that all this was occurring during the 2000–2002 financial crisis with the 9/11 bombing in between. But, of course, I knew better than to divest at that point in my life.

To put numbers to this illustration, let's look at Chart 1 at the back of this book where the value of the hypothetical illustration dropped from $365,000 in December 2000 down to $250,000. At this point in time many people would have pulled out of the stock market and stopped investing. They would have incurred a $115,000 loss, which would have taken them over 10 years to recover in the market. But if they would have continued to invest during the downturn from 2001–2003, by December 2006 the account would be worth $529,000.

A market drop also occurred in 2008–2009. Many people panicked and sold out at a loss. Using Chart 1, their account would have gone from $529,000 to $322,000 with a loss of $207,000. But the prudent investor who continued investing would have been handsomely rewarded over the next 12 years with over $2 million.

There will always be excuses, challenges, or reasons not to invest in the stock market. But the sooner you take the leap, the sooner you will begin to see your net worth grow. And the key is diversification, which will be explored in the next section.

Bottom Line: *Investing in the stock market is investing in the world—the companies founded by hard-working people who produce the goods and services that fuel our global economy (i.e., in the capitalistic way).*

Chapter 4

DIVERSIFICATION —

THE KEY TO INVESTMENT

SUCCESS

HOW WOULD YOU like to be served the same meal day after day, night after night? Especially if that meal consisted of only one dish? Even filet mignon would get old after a steady diet of it.

Investing in the stock market is much like developing a healthy, well-balanced diet. Consider your financial advisor as the "dietician" for your portfolio, helping you select those diverse funds and stocks and bonds that will assure you of a healthy return.

The concept of diversification in investing is a fundamental principle—simply spread your monies over a wide variety of sectors in order to avoid the risk of a substantial loss, especially if most of your money is in individual stocks or bonds when the market takes a downturn. Outside of a few known factors, it is nearly impossible to judge which stocks are going to turn out to be the next Tesla or Apple, so it makes sense to diversify.

"Most of the returns of the market over time are generated by a very small number of stocks. A 2019 study published in the

Journal of Financial Economics found that the best-performing 1% of stocks each year collectively account for the total gain of the stock market since 1926. If you choose to own only a fraction of the more than 3,500 publicly traded stocks in the U.S., what are the odds of picking exactly the right ones? Very small, probably similar to winning a lottery ticket. If you decide to invest in virtually all of the publicly listed stocks through a total stock market index fund, however, the odds that you will hold tomorrow's biggest winners are essentially 100%."[13]

Therefore, the total stock market index fund might be your best choice. Even so, after the Great Recession of 2008–2009, some financial experts suggested that investors should use some tactical maneuvers as well. This is known as "timing the market," which means to buy or sell investments to grow your portfolio. But this is not easy to do, and novices or day traders can get themselves in trouble, buying and selling at the wrong times. This is why I am continually encouraging people to engage the services of a licensed financial advisor and team. Even then, we are not prophets!

We do, however, have the advantage of years of experience and study, and this book is intended to help you avoid many of the mistakes common among beginning investors.

AN "APPLE" A DAY?

One of the largest holdings in any growth mutual fund or exchange traded fund (ETF) is Apple.[1] (Take a look at its growth record over the past five years on Chart 3 at the back of this book.) If China told Apple that tomorrow they could no longer market or sell cell phones, iPads, or computers in that country, what would happen to Apple's stock price? Right! It could be reduced by 50%.

[1] See author disclosure on copyright page.

If Apple represents 50% of your $500,000 stock portfolio, your net worth just dropped by $125,000. (Incidentally, I suggest that my clients never place more than 20% of their portfolio in any one stock. This way, a 50% decline in that stock's value will only have a 10% effect on the value of the total portfolio.) You can't worry about what you can't control, but you can protect against the damage with a little insurance. And your best insurance is diversification.

Stick with me while I draw you a picture of how diversification, plus wise allocation of funds, can minimize investment risk and bring peace to you and your family.

Consider Customer X, referred to us by his accountant, who had 100% of his investment capital in one stock that had appreciated significantly to a large, seven-digit figure. We devised a plan to unwind the stock over a five-year period, using a Charitable Remainder Annuity Trust (CRAT) to mitigate the taxes. The contribution to the CRAT is tax-deductible, using a special formula that calculates the tax benefit. In addition, when the trust CRAT sells the stock, there are no capital gains taxes to the stockholder, known as the grantor, and no federal estate tax.

Inside the CRAT, when we invested in various mutual funds early on, then transitioned to ETFs, the stock became less than 10% of the investor's holdings. The CRAT requires a 5% to 12% distribution to the grantor. In this case, the grantor took a 12% distribution to be able to gift his children. When this stockholder passed away, the charity was paid their 10%, and we are currently distributing the remainder to his grandchildren. We never had to invade the principal to make the 12% distribution. Plus, we had purchased life insurance that enabled the 10% monies paid to charity to be returned to the family, tax-free. A success story of the benefits of diversification and tax planning to preserve the gains and enrich the family for future generations, *and* to benefit charity. A win-win!

On the other hand, Customer Y (husband and wife) was also transferred to us from another firm. Their account contained over seventy-five individual stocks, with no one stock representing more than 2% of their portfolio. The account had made no gains for these clients over the past several years. We discovered that their portfolio had neither been rebalanced nor recalibrated to exclude certain non-performing sectors such as oil and commodities. After some sell-off and re-investing in *fewer* stocks, plus adding some sector ETFs and a couple of index ETFs, the results have been more than satisfactory.

Since every client's needs are unique, these two cases highlight the necessity of working with experts in the field of finance to know when and how to diversify. That being said, diversification is best achieved by what we call "rebalancing"—something your financial advisor should review for you annually.

REBALANCING YOUR PORTFOLIO

As the world turns, bringing changes every day, so, the world of finance shifts and evolves as well. With new discoveries in science and technology, lifestyle changes, new businesses developing, others merging, and still others going bankrupt and closing their doors forever, the financial world responds accordingly. Hence, market highs and lows. It would take a genius—or a biblical prophet—to accurately forecast what the future holds. Meanwhile, those of us in the field do know some ways to help those needing financial assistance in preparing for the future.

One, as we have mentioned, is the annual review. Sitting down with your advisor and team, you will have an opportunity to take a fresh look at your portfolio in view of changing circumstances. At this time, your advisor may suggest selling some stocks and buying others.

For example, if you had started out investing in a growth fund at $50 per month but were able to increase the amount as you progressed in business, that growth fund may now be worth over $100,000. At that point, we suggest you add a value ETF and a mid-cap ETF. (More about this later in this chapter.)

Rebalancing accomplishes several things:

- Makes sure you don't have too much money in one industry segment, such as Big Tech, energy, or healthcare.
- Ensures that you don't have too much money in one stock or bond.
- Provides liquidity when you need it. (Extremely important for retirees.)

We also try to keep two years of Required Minimum Distribution (RMD) of IRA accounts in short-term bonds and money market accounts. The required RMD begins at age 72. You will want to avoid having to sell any holdings when they are down over 40%. If you anticipate that you will need money in the next couple of years—i.e., car repair, new roof, emergency fund—always keep that money liquid. Over my forty-two-year career, I have seen too many people having to sell a piece of property, a stock, or a bond in order to meet a short-term need at a huge loss. Remember: It takes twice as long to recover a 20% loss as it did to make the same amount.

MARKET CAPITALIZATION

We owe much of the freedom we enjoy as a nation, not only to the Pilgrims, who left the tyranny of Europe and landed at Plymouth Rock to consecrate this country to the worship of God, but also to the concept of capitalism. As Dr. Milton Friedman famously said, "The typical state of mankind is tyranny, servitude, and misery....Political freedom clearly came along with the free market and the development of capitalist institutions."[14]

Those "capitalist institutions," such as Big Tech, automobile, and utility companies, are the engine that now drive our economy. As investors, we need to know something of what oils and fuels the engine. In the words of Eric Rosenberg, "A company's real value is the stock price times the number of shares outstanding. If a company has 100,000 shares trading at $10 each, the market capitalization, commonly called *market cap,* is $1 million. This is the number used to differentiate small-, mid-, and large-cap stocks."[15]

Let's take a moment to check out each of these investment possibilities, keeping in mind your personal goals and needs:

SMALL-CAP
Companies with Market Cap Less than $2 Billion

Every company starts here for obvious reasons. Just because these businesses are small doesn't mean small-cap stocks are undesirable or unimportant. In fact, there is more opportunity for these companies to grow faster and return money on your investment quicker. But they are also likely to be more volatile and riskier than mid- or large-cap stocks. But hang on for the ride! The growth possibilities can be exciting!

MID-CAP
Companies with Market Cap from $2 Billion to $10 Billion

Mid-cap stocks are the balance wheel for investors, balancing risk and reward. With room to grow, these companies can take off, allowing you to make a pretty penny on your investment. In addition, they attract larger companies that may desire takeovers, mergers, and other consolidation. You will definitely want to include some mid-cap stocks in your investment future, further fattening your portfolio.

LARGE-CAP
Companies with Market Cap of $10 Billion or More

Large-cap companies are the big guys, whose reputation for stability and endurance precedes them. These companies have the capital to advertise heavily, thus making their products a household name. They offer the "blue chip stocks" that everyone wants but may not be able to afford. Being large, however, makes them less flexible and less likely to grow. But the return on large-cap stocks is more dependable, and you will be the envy of small-cap investors.

INTERNATIONAL AND GLOBAL STOCKS
Foreign Ownerships (Asia, Europe) and
Emerging Markets (India, Brazil, etc.)

These stocks are relatively new areas in the past forty years, primarily due to the Internet. The information is easily accessible. The best way to purchase these is through either an ETF or mutual fund due to currency risks.

From this outline, you can see the advantages and disadvantages of each segment of stock market options. Unless you have plenty of money and don't mind taking risks, it is always wise to balance your portfolio with a good mix.

A DICTIONARY OF INVESTMENT OPTIONS
(and How to Apply Them)

Having worked in the field of finance for so long, I often forget that others may not be as familiar with our lingo, especially our abbreviations and acrostics. Throughout this book, I have attempted to spell them out for you, but in case we missed some, here is a handy guide, with tips on how to utilize them.

Bond: A bond is like a mortgage in reverse. Instead of paying an amount regularly, you collect on monies you have loaned to a government or institution. This is also known as fixed income.

Cash: The safest investment, relatively steady. It is best to invest in an interest-paying savings account. Keep in mind, however, that most banks offer low interest.

Commodities: A tangible asset—gold, silver, precious metals, oil, etc.—that can be traded. Rarely do you have to take physical possession of them.

Dividends: Cash payments regularly made to stockholders from the earnings of companies in which the stockholders are invested. These earnings are generated by products or services provided by the companies.

ETF (Exchange Traded Fund): A group of securities you buy and sell through your broker on the stock exchange (NYSE—New York Stock Exchange; S&P 500; NASDAQ). Most ETFs own over 100 different companies in different industries. They are available on almost all asset classes. As Jeremy Siegel says, "Exchange-traded funds (ETFs) are the most innovative and successful new financial instruments since stock index futures contracts debuted two decades earlier."[16]

Futures: A bit of a gamble, since this involves speculating on the future price of an asset. This requires the prospective owner to agree to buy and sell an asset at a prearranged price and by a future date.

Mutual Fund: These entities have been around since 1924 (Massachusetts Investors Trust). Mutual funds are a good way to create diversity with a small amount of money. Most funds hold numerous stocks or bonds. They are assembled with varying degrees of risk and sector rotations. The downfall of mutual funds is that the way they have to buy and sell holdings could cause a large taxable event. That's why it is best to own these inside of an IRA account. You can only buy or sell at the 4 p.m. closing price.

Real Estate: Ownership of physical property (though you would not count your own home as an investment property since you will be living there). The exception would be those who buy houses to remodel and flip, living in the house during the preparation to sell. Rental properties, commercial real estate, etc. could provide a great source of income as well as growth, but remember to consider maintenance and repair, not to mention the time involved, when deciding whether this would be a wise investment.

Stocks: Shares in a company, where you become part owner (a stockholder) of that company. (Remember: The difference between stocks and bonds is that with stocks, you are an owner; with bonds, you are a loaner.) While large companies are usually safer, they could also go bankrupt just like any company due to some unexpected natural or man-made calamity. Think Enron, General Motors, American Airlines, and AIG. Smaller, newly formed entities may have a higher risk factor, but also a greater growth potential.

You may decide to invest in stocks on your own, but if you decide to go it alone without the advice of a broker or financial advisor, you run the risk of betting on the wrong horse! With market volatility, any one stock can perform well one week and bottom out the next. That is why I continue to hammer the need for inexperienced investors to seek out wise counsel, preferably a team approach. If you decide to go this route, you may be advised to invest in ETFs or mutual funds, which provide the diversification necessary for a healthy portfolio.

. . .

A MODERN-DAY PRODIGAL SON

I have just reviewed a couple's portfolio, discussing some wealth management ideas with them on how best to give away some of their wealth to their son and daughter—especially in view of the younger child's (their son's) poor decision-making skills.

After much discussion, it was decided that they would give each child $100,000 now, filing a gift tax return since the gift exceeded $15,000, the maximum allowed without filing a return and lowering their $11-plus million exemption.

Shortly after this meeting, the daughter called me to open an investment account for her. Meanwhile, the son took off for Las Vegas and gambled away his share. With expensive hotels, prostitutes, and booze, he ran up a bill of $150,000. In no time, he was threatened with a lawsuit if he did not pay up in a few days.

The next step was the dreaded phone call to his dad. Even with the reservations about his son's lack of good judgment, the father had never expected things to get this bad! Luckily for his son, this man had a prosperous business and was a savvy investor. One call to me, and we wired the funds to the casino and hotel and paid the debt in full.

The homecoming was not quite like the story of the prodigal son in the Bible, where the father ran to meet his son while he was still a good way down the road, embracing him and then killing the fattened calf for a big celebration. Instead, the son in our story was met with a severe reprimand and new ground rules. While his parents forgave him, they also scolded him for not taking his responsibilities seriously. For the next few years, he would have to prove himself worthy of their trust.

He would work third shift at the factory at minimum wage, plus weekends at a restaurant, until his debt was repaid. As time went by, as a reward for his responsible work record, his father promoted him to third-shift supervisor, and after four long years, the debt was paid off. Now came the reward! At a surprise 25th birthday party, his father said, "Son, you can say goodbye to the third shift. I am promoting you to plant manager, and if you continue to do well, I will offer you stock options at age 30! Let the party begin!"

Although this story is fictionalized, it is my take on the "Parable of the Prodigal Son" in the Bible (see Luke 15:11–24). Some version of this scenario happens nearly every day—and with a variety of endings, some not so happy:

- Son is kidnapped and murdered in Las Vegas after the parents pay off a ransom that far exceeds the original gift.
- Son ends up destitute on the streets of Las Vegas, L.A., or San Francisco, and dies of a drug overdose, too embarrassed to talk to his parents.
- Parents disown their son and tell him never to darken their door again.

The voice of reason comes in different forms. But where you begin does not necessarily mean where you will finish. If you will heed the wisdom of financial counselors, who have studied, applied sound financial principles, and have also learned from their own mistakes, you can build your net worth and further ensure your future.

Bottom Line: *After you have considered each of the investment options available to you, it is wise to invest in a variety of asset classes (i.e., healthcare, transportation, real estate, etc.); in other words, diversify. A well-rounded portfolio will give you insurance against the probability of market fluctuations. And be sure to recalibrate each year with your financial team!*

Chapter 5

QUICKSAND:

GOOD DEBT/BAD DEBT

The rich rule over the poor, and the borrower is servant to the lender. (Proverbs 22:7)

The most crippling disease in the United States is not cancer, not heart disease, not alcoholism—it is spenders' anonymous.
–John F. Savage, CLU, Toledo, Ohio

STANDING IN MY daughter Sarah's backyard, we looked out over the five gorgeous green acres she and her husband had recently purchased not far from my home. In the distance, majestic trees—maple, oak, walnut, cherry—stood sentinel, as if guarding the perimeter. Behind us was the modest farmhouse that presided over this impressive acreage. But the house was needing a facelift. The remodel would require some time—and quite a bit of money.

As is often the case in our family, our conversation shifted to finances. Curious as to what she might have gleaned from our frequent discussions on the topic, I asked Sarah, "What is good debt versus bad debt?"

She didn't miss a beat. "Good debt purchases an asset that appreciates in value—like this place," she said with a sweeping gesture. "Bad debt is just the opposite. The purchase depreciates in value."

That's my girl, I thought, nodding in approval. Even in times like these—unexpected disasters, global unrest, financial uncertainty—real estate investing is still a pretty safe bet.

A few years earlier, Sarah and her husband, Daniel, had started their life together as newlyweds. At the time, Daniel was a schoolteacher and Sarah, a nurse. With their combined incomes, they were able to save enough money for a down payment on a small house. When the children started arriving, Sarah decided to opt for stay-at-home mom rather than a nursing career. With their income now slashed in half, this meant selling their house and downsizing to apartment living.

"Don't rent too long, though," I cautioned them. "When you pay rent, you're only building somebody else's net worth."

When my son-in-law advanced to the highest-paying school in the district and his income increased by 20%, they soon saved enough to buy a ranch house. Of course, they were frugal, spent money wisely, and didn't rack up big debt. They were also socking away $50 per month in a growth fund, along with Daniel's state teachers' retirement account.

Eight years later, they sold that house, made $70,000 on it, and bought another for $195,000, using their profit from the sale and some tax refunds. They are remodeling a bit and adding another room, after which their new home will be valued at $300,000. When you figure the value of the house, plus investments, Daniel will have increased his net worth by over six digits. And all this on a schoolteacher's salary!

So, how did they do it? What was their game plan? For one thing, they avoided "bad debt."

"BAD" DEBT

Debt is a lot like any bad habit. It is so easy to acquire a credit card. So easy to fall for the "90-day-same-as-cash" routine. So easy to get a third line of credit on your house. So hard to pay it back! For example, my wife and I never bought a new car until I was past 50 years of age. Why? Because this is one item that depreciates the moment you drive it off the showroom floor or out of the auto lot. The other two high-risk purchases are recreational vehicles and boats.

The following are some areas of "bad" debt that you should avoid like the plague or the 2020 pandemic, COVID-19:

AUTO LOANS:

I recently bought my wife a 2017 Subaru Outback, trading in a 2010 Ford Edge with 110,000 miles on it. I had the option of $1,000 cashback or 0% financing over forty-eight months. With my investments averaging 8% return over the past twenty years, it was pretty easy math in my case. When it comes to your situation, you'll have to do the math, too, and decide which would be the better option.

And never add the balance of your old car loan to a new loan on a newer vehicle. For the first few years, you will owe more than the new vehicle is worth.

BUY HERE/PAY HERE AUTO SALES:

You may be fresh out of school, trying to live independently, and need transportation to work. You have bad credit and have not been able to get a loan anywhere. Suddenly you spot a sign at a corner auto sales lot: *Buy Here/Pay Here!* Wow! Too good to be true? You'd better believe it!

Here are the pros and cons of "dealing" with this kind of dealership:

Pros:
- No credit required.
- Easy to purchase a vehicle.
- Dealer is willing to accept older trade-ins.

Cons:
- High interest rates (four to five times higher than traditional loans).
- Will track your car.
- Odd payment requirements (monthly, weekly, in-person).
- May not report to credit bureaus.
- Limited selection of vehicles.
- High down payment.[17]

You may buy some piece of junk for a super-low price, but all you will be doing is purchasing someone else's headache. When the 30-day warranty runs *out,* you are likely to run *into* trouble with some major repair. Not only that, but think of the owner of the lot as a loan shark; it's like borrowing money from the Mafia! Miss one payment, and the dealer will repossess without batting an eye.

CREDIT CARDS:

There is good news and bad news where credit cards are concerned. (I'll tell you the good news later.) Never—and I do mean *never*—use a credit card for any of the following:

- to purchase an eighty-inch-screen TV to watch the Super Bowl
- to finance your higher education
- to buy furniture, which will depreciate by 50% the minute you bring it home
- to put a down payment on a boat or car
- to pay for an expensive vacation, which you will later have to repay, plus interest. After the seaside sunsets and the ocean-view luxury hotel room, all you will have to look forward to when you get home is paying off that massive debt.

RENT TO OWN:

This is worse than Buy Here/Pay Here. Don't do it! With an interest rate of over 20%, it is like buying two TVs and getting only one.

MULTI-LEVEL MARKETING

Early in 2000, after the Y2K panic—the fear of the electric grid going black, banks failing, computers shutting down—we realized that the turn of the century had passed without a hitch. It was then I received a call from a fellow church member who wanted to meet with me over lunch regarding an investment idea.

In fact, he wanted to liquidate a certain amount of money from his investments and enter into an alternative investment called Purchase Plus. It took me a while to understand the alternative investment idea. "Everybody wins," he assured me. "You sell the plan to several people who sign up others under their name and yours. Each of you gets a share of all profits."

When I realized that he was proposing a multi-level marketing plan, I turned him down. Man, was he disappointed! He knew I had plenty of contacts and could likely sign up a large number of people.

He continued to press, and I countered by asking for the following:

1. An audited financial statement
2. An operating agreement

His refusal to honor my request sent up some red flags, and I warned, "I don't think this is a good idea." He was not satisfied with my line of reasoning. Unhappy with the way our meeting had ended, I decided to do some more investigating. The next time my youngest son, Adam, and I were in Westerville, a suburb of Columbus and the home office of this operation, I sent him on a tour of the facility. After listening to the guide's spiel, my son said, "Dad, this is a rip-off!"

Later, I sent my daughter Rachel to an MLM party. She, too, was told: "Everyone makes money. You can't lose!"

She came back with the same impression as Adam: "Sounded like a scam to me, Dad."

Meanwhile, my client had made good on his decision to invest in the questionable company. Worse still, many in our church had invested a total of hundreds of thousands of dollars. At an elders' meeting, I had tried to warn them too. "I think this is a mistake. We may not be promoting this as a church, but people in the community who think highly of you will follow suit, and it's too risky. I don't advise it."

Like my client, they didn't listen. In fact, some were so upset with me for suggesting that they shouldn't invest in the MLM, they cut ties with me. Eventually, the plan was shut down by the state attorney general. Relationships were broken. Bankruptcies declared. Families disrupted, including my client's family, whose wife almost left him for failing to consult her before making his decision and, thus, losing all their money. Most heartbreaking of all, our church split. All because of greed and poor decisions.

If you are ever approached to participate in an MLM scheme, run the other way. But before you do, you might want to do your own research and ask for the documents I requested. If the "salesman" fails to produce them, you'll know I was right.

As Dave Ramsey writes, "We live among a bunch of people who are deeply in debt and have no money saved because their emotions were tricked. Just like drug addicts, people have been conned into believing that happiness will come with the next purchase. So, Daddy works hundreds of overtime hours and Mommy works forty-plus hours a week, all in the name of STUFF...

"You can get out of debt, save money and get on a budget, but until your intellect forces your emotions and your spirit to accept that STUFF does not equal CONTENTMENT, your finances will always feel stressed. At our office we counsel every week with folks who are making $25,000 per year as well as folks making $250,000 per year. These people share a common problem: they all suffer from some level of "stuffitis," or the worship of stuff. Change your focus and change your life for the better."[18]

On this point, I agree with our friend Dave Ramsey. On the other hand, I believe there is such a thing as "good" debt.

"GOOD" DEBT"

I am happy to report now on that good news I promised you. As long as there is return on the dollar or value received, some debt could actually be construed as investment. Consider student loans, for example.

STUDENT LOANS

The diploma received at the end of four long years spent pouring over books is the reward of an investment in your future. Some employers will pay your student loan as part of your employee contract. In 2019, for example, in a year of high employment, this concept ramped up considerably as an incentive for recruiting top-notch employees.

Many high schools offer college-bound students the opportunity to take college courses at no expense during their junior and senior years. It is possible to complete nearly two years of college, earning an associate degree by the time you graduate high school. In Ohio, a branch of Ohio State University, along with North Central State College, offers degrees at a fraction of the cost of on-campus living. In other words, if you live at home and commute to classes, plus work a few hours at an after-school job, you could earn an education or business degree for less than $15,000. No student loan! Of course, there is the option to serve our country via Army, Navy, Marine Corps, Air Force, Space Force, or the National Guard, and let Uncle Sam pick up the tab for your college degree.

Rule of thumb: If your student loan enables you to receive a degree that increases your income by 30% to 40% (i.e., you advance from nurse-to-nurse practitioner or schoolteacher to principal), and as long as your loan is not more than 50% of your pay increase, the student loan makes financial sense.

A word of warning: If you default on your federally generated student loan, the amount owed—up to 50% or more—will be deducted from your Social Security check upon retirement until the loan is paid back.

CREDIT CARDS

In my opinion, credit cards are a necessary evil in today's economy, but acceptable if the balance is paid in full at the end of each month or if more-than-minimum payments are made. If used properly, they can be a means of accumulating air miles for your next trip or buying your spouse a birthday gift with the points. Keep in mind that, once again, interest rates are usually high—12% to 20%—so you will want to pay off or pay down as quickly as possible.

A few years ago, my wife and I vacationed at an all-inclusive resort in Cancun, Mexico. We both loved walks on the powdered-sugar sands of the beach. Enjoyed looking out over the turquoise waters, dotted with white sailboats. Savored the burnt-orange sunsets over seaside dinners. And every day, I swam in the ocean. Inevitably, I ingested some salt water in the process.

Several days into our ten-day vacation, I began to feel ill. The resort doctor checked me, diagnosed a stomach virus, and gave me a shot to halt the severe vomiting with the warning that if this didn't stop in a couple of hours, I should go to a hospital to be treated for dehydration. Two hours later, there was no change, and we called a taxi for the hour-long, roller-coaster ride to the nearest hospital, my wife still in her bathing suit and cover-up!

Upon arriving, we quickly found that I was not the only patient in need of care. I was one of a long line of very sick people—same symptoms as mine—all of whom had to be registered before being admitted. We later learned that some of the surrounding resorts had inadvertently released their sewage into the ocean, polluting the entire area.

When it was finally my wife's turn to supply the needed information for me, she was told that we would have to pay in advance. The bill? $5,000, later adjusted to $10,000 since my care included an overnight stay!

Fortunately, when traveling, I carry a credit card with a generous credit limit. Highly recommended for just such emergencies. The good news is that, between our health insurance and travel insurance, most of the exorbitant expenses were reimbursed.

TAXES

Even if, for some reason, you do not owe money to a bank, credit card company, or finance company, come January 1, you are definitely in debt to the Internal Revenue Department of the United

States Government. In fact, the government now takes over half of my income annually!

Most Americans never calculate the amount of taxes they actually pay. Here is a rundown of percentages of my gross income I owe the government each year:

- Federal tax: 20%–30%
- State tax: 7%
- Real Estate Tax: 1%–10% of property value (depending upon the state where you live)
- Social Security and Medicare: 13.85%
- State Sales Tax (Ohio): 5.75%
- Local School and City Tax: 2%

The IRS is ruthless when it comes to people who don't pay their taxes. It may take them three years or so to catch up with you, but eventually they will. The infamous mob boss Al Capone didn't go to jail for theft or even murder. He was finally convicted—of all things—of tax evasion!

I once worked with a small business owner who ran into some tax trouble down the line. After gathering his returns and other pertinent information as we always do in determining how best to help a client with their financial and retirement plans, something just didn't add up. I couldn't quite figure out where he was making his profit. A few months later, the state closed down his business for failure to pay the state sales tax. He had collected the monies from customers, yet never forwarded it to the proper authorities. Result: His wife divorced him, and he fled the state.

As much as we may despise paying taxes—and there does need to be some restructuring or changes made in our tax system—we "owe" our fair share for the privilege of living in the greatest country in the world!

As mentioned, the Bible has quite a lot to say on this subject.

Once, a group of Sadducees—some of the religious elites of the day—tried to trap Jesus on the matter of taxes:

> "So tell us, then, what you think. Is it proper for us Jews to pay taxes to Caesar or not?"
>
> Jesus knew the malice that was hidden behind their cunning ploy and said, "Why are you testing me? ... Show me one of the Roman coins." So they brought him a silver coin used to pay the tax. "Now, tell me, whose head is on this coin and whose inscription is stamped on it?"
>
> "Caesar's," they replied.
>
> Jesus said, "Precisely, for the coin bears the image of the emperor Caesar. Well, then, you should pay the emperor what is due to the emperor. But because you bear the image of God, give back to God all that is God's." (Matthew 22:17–21 TPT)

REAL ESTATE

You already know my position on real estate. Although in purchasing a home, there is usually a hefty down payment required and monthly mortgage payments, careful planning can make this one of the safest and best "debts" you could incur.

In the beginning of this chapter, you met one of my daughters, Sarah, and her husband, Daniel. Now let me introduce you to my other daughter, Rachel, and her husband, Bo. They have a similar real estate success story. Both couples purchased homes shortly after marriage.

Rachel graduated from Ohio State University in 2005 with a degree in Dance Education. While she was a student at OSU in Columbus, I bought a house where she could live and serve as managing landlady, renting out rooms to her girlfriends. This money covered the mortgage and utilities. When she graduated,

I sold the house in Columbus for $10,000 profit after expenses and gave her the profit for managing the property.

She and Bo married soon thereafter. During their college days, both had worked as servers in a local restaurant and had saved all their tip money. This money covered their honeymoon expenses. Within a month after their marriage and with the $10,000 from the sale of the house in Columbus, they bought a small, three-bedroom home in Mansfield for $71,400. Neither their mother nor I had to co-sign.

The house needed some work—updating and landscaping. But having been brought up on a dairy farm, Bo was quite handy and with a little elbow grease, they managed to increase the value of the house, even during the Great Recession of 2008–2009!

Bo soon landed a job in construction and Rachel began working for me, administrating 401(k) plans. Their combined income? Less than $65,000 per year. Still, they made regular payments on their mortgage and Bo's student loans, as well as continuing to match their 401(k) plans.

A few years later, they moved from Mansfield to Butler, the village where Rachel was born, and bought a much larger house with a small barn on a one-acre lot. This purchase, plus their 401(k)/IRA accounts, allowed them to increase their net worth. Today, with five children under the age of 12, they are still able to invest monies into their IRA accounts, bringing their combined income to around $75,000 annually.

Over the next six months, they plan to remodel their house, with Bo and some friends doing most of the work. They will be converting the attic into a fourth bedroom for the two older boys. This addition will increase the value of their home by $10,000 to $20,000. Another success story!

• • •

My daughters' stories have been told to help you understand a major concept: **You can never recover time lost.**

Both daughters' husbands have student loans.

Both daughters' families have car loans.

Both daughters have bought and sold houses for profit and redeposited monies into larger homes and property with larger mortgages. But this is good debt! The result has been an increase in their net worth. They didn't stop investing in the stock market to pay off mortgages or car payments. They continued to do both!

Because of their income, number of children, and tax-deductible mortgage interest, they pay very little state or federal income tax. Remember: Anything you can do *legally* to minimize your taxes will automatically build your net worth if that money is invested in stocks or in your home.

My family knows that the more money they can invest between the ages of 20 and 30, the less they will have to invest between the ages of 50 and 60. If my daughters and their husbands had waited to invest until after they paid off their mortgages and car loans, neither couple would have had any monies to invest in the stock market, where long-term benefits will result.

Bottom Line: *Once too much bad debt sucks you in, you're in quicksand unless someone throws you a lifeline. As one investment expert once said, "People don't plan to fail, they fail to plan."*

Chapter 6

MIND YOUR OWN BUSINESS

A leader is one who knows the way, goes the way,
and shows the way.
–John C. Maxwell

The world is moved along not only by the mighty
shoves of its heroes, but also by the aggregate of the
tiny pushes of each honest worker.
–Helen Keller

LEST YOU THINK I was born with "a silver spoon in my mouth,"
as the old saying goes, think again. My mother drilled in me a
superior work ethic. From her example and my own fear of becoming the loser that Principal Porter predicted, I, too, have
worked hard all my life. And may I remind you that the company
I "inherited" from my dad when he retired was not given to me.
I continued to pay a set amount of money until the death of my
parents. (Actually, the total amount was ten times more than the

company was worth at the time—not knowing my parents would live into their nineties.) In the process, I learned how to build a thriving business in a tiny town during several economic fluctuations.

Although not everyone is cut out to be their own boss and run a company, owning and managing my business has been, for me, the best investment I have ever made! My team and I determine our own goals and vision, decide which products to market, what fees to charge within certain government parameters, which attorneys and CPA will advise us, and what auditor and compliance firm we will choose to oversee our books.

Because I am not a territorial kind of person, I am willing to share my "secrets" with you so you also may enjoy success.

BUILDING A SUCCESSFUL BUSINESS
Some of these tips may come as a surprise to you, so be prepared.

1: YOUR WORK ETHIC

As the head of your company, you set the tone for how your business will operate. What you expect from your colleagues and employees, you yourself must first model.

HUMILITY: Very few business leaders are willing to ask for advice, but success starts here. There is a proverb in the Bible that deals with this: "*Pride goes before destruction, a haughty spirit before a fall*" (Proverbs 16:18). If you begin your business thinking you know it all, you are more likely to fail than to succeed. So, when you need outside counsel, don't hesitate to ask for it.

Recently, I met with the CEO of one of the only publicly held companies in our area. The purpose of the meeting was to ask him what he looked for in a company he was considering for purchase or merger. The answer was surprising. It was not cash flow.

It was not a defective product or a personnel problem. It was culture! For example, if he walked into the restroom of a prospective business he was considering purchasing and found that it was not clean, that told him something about the kind of culture the company operates within. "You can change the production methods," he said. "You can change the suppliers or other aspects of the operation, but you can't change the culture." Good point—and one I would have missed had I been reluctant to seek advice.

DISCIPLINE: Since no one sets the hours except you, it would be best for you as the boss to be known for your diligence and long hours on the job rather than for long lunch hours. For the first thirty years of my career, I was the first to arrive on the job and the last to leave, but it is also true that much business can be conducted over a meal—or on the golf course!

PASSION: Unless you are passionate about your work, no one else will be—neither coworkers nor clients. Many times, after conducting a 401(k) seminar with factory workers, construction workers, and other small business owners in the audience, I hear this comment: "Wow! You really believe in your service, don't you? Never heard such passion and enthusiasm in a business meeting!"

The opposite is also true. If you can't talk about your product or service with passion, your prospective customer will sense it. For example, if you're merely reading from a script over the phone to sell a product, it's not going to happen. But if you are genuinely passionate in describing the benefits of your product or service, your potential client will be intrigued and want to know more.

Colleagues have also wanted to know how I can sell so many 401 (k) plans. The answer is simple: "You have not because you ask not." Many people lose sales because they are afraid to ask, fearing the answer will be no. I have had to overcome my own insecurities and fear of rejection caused by my father and other personal challenges. As a result, I no longer hesitate to approach my dentist, my eye doctor, the hardware store owner, the grocer, the owner of the concrete company who built my building in 2000, etc. and ask for their business. Very few have turned me down.

PRIORITIZATION AND ORGANIZATION: The words speak for themselves. There are obvious organizational needs in a start-up business or even when updating an established company like mine. But it was the prioritizing that gave me the biggest challenge—and continues to this day. The priorities of God, family, and business. Keeping my priorities in that order is difficult. It's a challenge for me to go to work and not think about my family. It's a challenge for me to go home at night and leave my work behind. And even in church, it's a challenge to stay focused on worshiping God and not let my mind wander to some family issue or problem at the office I need to resolve. If this is your situation, don't give up! Stick with it! The last word? God once spoke to a pastor friend in these pointed words: "If you take care of My business, I'll take care of yours!"

YOUR TEAM: Without a doubt, the team you assemble must be composed of compatible people. Anything less spells disaster. So, build your team carefully and prayerfully. If you don't enjoy working together, you will encounter friction and factions at every turn, sabotaging the outcome of many a project.

A big key here is to duplicate yourself. The best way to do that is to use the apprentice approach. Have your new associates follow you through a typical business day and listen to you make presentations to your clients as well as have them develop client presentations. When it is their turn to sell, write the new associates some scripts but insist they rephrase the message in their own words so that the financial ideas do not appear "canned." Encourage them to familiarize themselves with every product—from life insurance to IRA accounts to 401(k) plans, so they can explain them with a passion to match your own. One thing I insist upon is that my reps never answer a potential client or existing client's question with "I don't know." If they don't know the answer, I suggest that they reply, "I'll get back to you tomorrow." Then I encourage them to follow up with a phone call within twenty-four hours.

2: YOUR MARKETING PLAN

You can have the greatest ideas in the world, but if nobody knows about them, it would be extremely difficult to sell them. We tried billboards to advertise our business but dropped that contract after one year. Too pricey and not enough return on our investment.

In this technological age, social media is the current go-to marketing tool. Be sure you create a website that attracts viewers. What are the hot button words and images that will draw customers to your product or service? Be creative or hire a firm that will produce the needed results.

If you hire an outside ad agency, make sure they capture not only your concept but your enthusiasm for what you are offering the public. Our number-one growth secret is referrals. Not billboards. Not a website. Not social media. It's satisfied customers telling family, friends, and business associates about our services.

3: YOUR CONTINUING EDUCATION

To keep abreast of our changing times, you will want to attend management seminars specific to your business. These are available in almost every city and will be one of the best investments of time and money you can make. One of the last financial seminars I attended, led by a consultant to some of the most successful financial service companies in the United States, gave me the inspiration for our 5D Process. I will continue to learn in this ever-evolving economic landscape. I would suggest you make that commitment too.

4: YOUR INSURANCE POLICY AGAINST FAILURE

Every successful business must fortify itself against the possibility of failure by ensuring recurring revenue. For example, in the year 2020—possibly because of the pandemic that year—Apple computer stock was making more money from the services they provide than from the product they sell. Interesting that the first few companies Warren Buffett bought were insurance companies! Why? These companies have recurring revenue and almost anything you buy today—home, car, health—requires insurance.

5: YOUR HOME AND PERSONAL LIFE

One of the top reasons people go out of business is lack of balance between work and family. It's what I call the Proverbs 11:1 rule: *"The LORD abhors dishonest scales, but accurate weights are his delight."* This wise saying is not only referring to a biblical merchant who used weighted scales in order to charge the customer unfairly, but it is calling our attention to a proper balance in life.

Early in our marriage—after my father's retirement and my acquisition of the company—my wife and I made the decision that when our children arrived, she would be a stay-at-home mom and I would bring home the bacon. Our children joined the family in record time—four kids in five years—and I was caught up in learning the business. To say that we were busy but blessed is an understatement. That balancing act was a continual challenge, but we were determined to make time for our growing family, and I did everything possible to spend quality time with my wife. If we couldn't manage those priorities, how did we expect to manage a business?

In all the years I have been in business, I have rarely received a thank-you card for my services. But just last month, I received my first phone call ever from a satisfied client, thanking me for helping with his portfolio of investments, along with estate and financial planning. "I wouldn't be where I am today without your help," he said. That was music to my ears. But knowing I am an honest businessman, using "honest scales" and bringing "delight" to the Lord trumps thank-you notes and satisfied customer calls!

ESB—FOUR LEVELS OF SUCCESS

Reading inspirational stories of biblical heroes, including the miracles of Jesus Himself, as well as the success of more contemporary entrepreneurs (see chapter 2), motivates us to make the most of our opportunities while we are on this earth. Even as a young man, I was given one of those opportunities, and I didn't want to miss the chance to "make something of myself," as my mother had encouraged me to do.

LEVEL 1: 1982–1995

In 1982, when my father retired at age 65, I signed a contract agreeing to pay so much per year in exchange for ownership of the company. The early '80s was a time when many changes were taking place in the industry.

Whole life insurance was being replaced by universal life, which transferred more of the risk of the interest/investment to the consumer. Also, defined benefit pension plans were being replaced by 401(k) plans, which meant that employers would require employees to share the responsibility for their retirement plans rather than assuming 100% of the burden—another risk factor for the consumer. At the same time, there was an evolution of investment products, including mutual funds and ETFs.

That meant back to school for me. I enrolled in two college courses to learn the new legal terminology and logistics of the 401(k) plans and sat in on some business practice management seminars.

When my mother, who had worked for the company for years, decided to join my dad in retirement (actually, I had to politely "encourage" her to leave—one of the toughest things I have ever had to do!), we hired an administrator for the 401(k) plans and purchased software to facilitate the crunching of numbers and to produce government required investing. At this point, we also hired my brother Lyle to service the ten health plans and, not long after that, a second administrator to help with high-deductible, self-insured health plans.

We have always marketed E.S. Beveridge and Associates, Inc. as a human resources (HR) support agency for both company-required plan and health insurance and employee benefits—a one-stop shop, saving HR departments both time and monies.

By 1995, we had grown from ten defined benefit pension plans to over fifty 401(k) plans and from ten health plans to over thirty. Revenue had increased five times!

LEVEL 2: 1995–2012

Still operating as one company, I gave my brother Lyle 40% ownership. During these years, we created our own 401(k) product record-keeping TPA (third-party administrator) firm and portfolio management system, all executed in-house. By now, we had cultivated over one hundred fifty 401(k) plans with eight employees.

This upsurge of business necessitated the hiring of a third and fourth sales associate—my son, Adam, and his friend, Preston Boyd. They were to help facilitate 401(k) enrollments and service our second and third mergers in Toledo, Ohio, and the Seattle and Tacoma, Washington, areas.

Unfortunately, Toledo turned out to be a disaster and Seattle was break-even. This was the result of several miscalculations on travel and logistics, plus some personnel problems. However, through these setbacks and failures, we learned valuable lessons on the importance of contracts and finding loyal, trustworthy sales associates.

In less than twenty years, our business grew to over 60 Health Plans and over 175 401(k) Plans, supporting eighteen families.

LEVEL 3: 2012–2019

Due to the major changes made by Obamacare to private doctors' practices and insurance payments, many doctors went to work for hospitals and closed their private practices. The insurance changes made it almost impossible to compete for reinsurance against such companies as Blue Cross, Blue Shield, Aetna, and Medical Mutual.

After some deliberations with our lawyers and accountants, we thought it best to divide the company into three sections. E.S. Beveridge Associates Inc. would now be identified as:

- ESB Wealth/Pro TPA (401(k) and profit-sharing plans)
- ESB Investments Inc. (personal retirement, estate planning, and wealth management)
- E.S. Beveridge Associates Inc. (health insurance, Medicare supplements, and long-term care insurance)

Our business shrank by 50% due to the number of physicians' plans we lost. But our net income rose because of increases in individual financial planning and lower labor costs. Recently, we added another 401(k) sales rep to our organization—one with a great résumé and catalog of contacts, mainly located outside of our immediate area. He is well qualified and displays a tremendous work ethic. This addition to our staff will bring another stream of referrals to our estate/individual retirement financial planning division.

I am continually on the lookout for people of character and proper qualifications to join our firm. Experience has proven that it is character, though, that often trumps qualifications.

LEVEL 4: 2019–2020

When I assumed ownership of the company in 1984, our total assets under management (AUM) was $2 to $3 million in annuities. My initial goal was to have twenty-five 401(k) plans and $50 million in assets within the first ten years. By 1995, a year shy of my goal, we had exceeded the goal with fifty 401(k) plans and close to $50 million in personal investment accounts and 401(k) plans. These totals were achieved in a community that had lost over 15,000 manufacturing jobs from 1974 to 2000, and several thousand more when a GM plant closed in 2011–2012!

Despite the loss of jobs in our North Central Ohio area of six counties, we grew to over $100 million in AUM by 2000, with over one hundred 401(k) plans. Today, our total AUM with all sales associates is $400 million with seventy 401(k) plans.

In June of 2020, we met to remodel our companies for a fourth time. This remodel was needed due in part to the pandemic, the CARES Act, and the ever-evolving technology, with robo-advisors for 401(k) plans/ individual accounts. Just ask a robo whether you should have a Roth IRA or a traditional IRA and watch it start smokin'! In addition, we changed our name to ESB W&I (wealth and investments).

Our strategy over the next several years is to continue our efforts with business owners/baby boomers but also to make sure they introduce us to their children, the millennials. In other words, we will prepare for the greatest transfer of wealth in history—estimated to be around $40 trillion-plus—from the present generation to younger generations. Following World War II, the population exploded, along with significant wealth, "roughly 70 percent of all disposable income, according to a 2015 report by *US News and World Report*."[19] This presents both positive and negative consequences. With this dramatic shift of income, depending upon the recipients and their understanding of how to handle wealth, there could be amazing opportunities for gaining even more...or sadly, for loss. Therefore, one of our challenges as a company is to educate the younger generations in money management and investment, one of the main reasons I have written this book.

We will utilize our 5D process to gather more personal individual clients as well as small business owners for whom we can provide financial and retirement planning, plus estate planning.

One of our new marketing strategies will be to ask small business owners, "When was the last time your accountant, lawyer, and financial advisor sat down together to discuss your business plan, your financial plan, your estate plan, your retirement plan?" Very few bring these important players to the table at the same time. Consequently, their plans are often helter-skelter.

Overall, the idea is to focus marketing on individuals first, 401(k) plans second—the reverse of our approach for the past thirty years.

And this is how a small business in a small town can grow twenty times greater than its humble beginnings.

• • •

Years ago, I ran across a book that captured the essence of a dilemma that is escalating in America with the shutdowns brought on by the COVID-19 pandemic. Written by Chuck Colson and Jack Eckerd, the book is titled *Why America Doesn't Work.* The content is as true today as when it was first published in 1991.

"People view work in many ways: as a necessary evil to keep bread on the table; as a means to a sizable bank account; as self-fulfillment and identity; as an economic obligation within society; as a means to a life of leisure. Yet none of these represents an adequate view of work that provides ongoing or complete satisfaction. We are more than material beings, more than social beings, and more than cogs in the machinery of work.

We are, above all, spiritual beings, and as such we need to rediscover the moral and spiritual significance for every area and aspect of our lives, including our work.

Why, then, should we work?

Because work gives expression to our creative gifts and thus fulfills our need for meaning and purpose. Because work is intrinsically good when done with the proper attitude and motive. Because we are commanded to exercise stewardship over the earth, participating in the work of Creation in a way that glorifies God. Because we are citizens of this earth and have certain responsibilities to our fellow citizens. It is this moral character of work that historically has been the very heart of the work ethic."[20]

It is this model, set out by Colson and Eckerd, that I want to teach my employees, colleagues, children, grandchildren, and all who are reading this book. And, if I'm smart, I will be sure to create a plan of succession that will ensure the success of my business long after I'm gone.

Bottom Line: *By using your God-given gifts and talents, along with humility, passion, dedication, and teamwork, you can build a successful business. But don't forget to create a succession plan that will allow the business to continue to succeed after your passing.*

Chapter 7

RETIREMENT IS *NOT* IN THE BIBLE

"So here I am today, eighty-five years old! I am still as strong today as the day that Moses sent me out; I'm just as vigorous to go out to battle now as I was then."
(Joshua 14:10–11)

MOSES LED HIS people out of Egyptian captivity at age 80. Caleb was 85 when he took a mountain, routed the enemy, and entered the Promised Land. Sarah was 90 when she gave birth to Isaac, the covenant child.

And I am writing this book at the age of 65 with the assistance of my ghostwriter who is 85! We intend to keep working until the Lord calls us home because, as our title suggests, neither the word *retirement* nor the concept is mentioned anywhere in the Bible.

In fact, before World War II, very few people—less than 1% of the population—considered retiring from the workplace. In 1936, the average male lived to be 56.6 years old; their female counterparts beat them by a few years, making it to 60.6 years. By 1960, the lifespan of the average male had increased to 69.7 years and for females, 73.1 years. Still, only about 10% of the population collected Social Security. By the year 2020, men and women were nearly neck and neck, their lifespans averaging 79 and 80 respectively. Still, considering financial preparation for retirement is a relatively new phenomenon in the twentieth and twenty-first centuries.

While it is best—physically, emotionally, and spiritually—to stay busy in our latter years, we also need to prepare financially and practically for that time when we are not producing income due to mandatory guidelines set by businesses (i.e., airline pilots, truck drivers, and surgeons). Sadly, the fact is that Social Security covers less than half the average retiree's costs of living, and a recent report shows that 40% of older Americans rely solely on Social Security for their income in their retirement years.[21]

According to a recent study, the chart below catalogs the dismal failure of citizens of the richest nation in the world to put away enough money to support themselves through the remainder of their lives. The following figures show how little prepared we are for our own future. Let me spell it out for you:

Between the ages of 32–37, some people have about $480 set aside in a retirement fund.

From ages 38–43: $4,200
From ages 44–49: $6,200
From ages 50–55: $8,000
From ages 56–61: $17,000

"The Economic Policy Institute (EPI) paints an even bleaker picture. Their data from 2013 reports that 'nearly half of families have no retirement account savings at all!'"[22] So, how much money do you actually need to live comfortably when you are no longer working?

NO MORE PAYCHECK? WHAT NOW?

You may be asking, "Will I run out of money before I die?" Not a particularly happy thought, but something nearly everyone entertains at some point along the way.

You only need to tally your cost-of-living expenses from the previous year to calculate a more realistic view of what you will require when you reach retirement age. And that does not include potential medical expenses or assisted living, as you may require more care in your latter years. A more accurate answer is dependent on four factors:

Where you are currently living or where you wish to relocate after retirement. For example, the cost of living in Richland County, Ohio, where I live, is quite different than if I were to move to the East or West Coast or near a body of water. Wherever you choose to live, your primary residence should be paid for by age 70 at the latest!

The amount of money you will need to supplement your pension (if you have one) and/or Social Security. The minimum target is $200,000. This would give you $1,000 per month above your other sources of income and should last as long as you live, if managed properly. I have clients who are living on this amount here in my county and enjoying a simple lifestyle, quite content to live within their means. Again, it depends on location, location, location, as they say in the real estate business.

Your health. For most senior citizens, their largest expenditure is health care. If you have no family member(s) who would be able to take care of you in your declining years, you would have to consider, at the least, an assisted living facility or in-home caregiver. And be sure your health insurance is up to date.

The amount of money you want to leave to your heirs or to a charity.

Even if your estimates fall short of your necessary goal, there is still something you can do to build a more secure future.

YOUR FINANCIAL "BUCKET LIST"

Some time ago, I ran across a little book that laid out in simple terms one of the best overall strategies (that I have found) for preparing for the second half of life. In his book, *The Bucket Plan: Protecting and Growing Your Assets for a Worry-Free Retirement,* Jason L. Smith suggests the following guidelines:

The "Now" Bucket: This is your safety net, your emergency fund, and the money used to cover living expenses or any large, planned expenses during the first one to two years of your retirement.

The "Soon" Bucket: Monies invested conservatively since you may need the returns "sooner" rather than "later." This plan helps reduce the risks associated with investing in a market known for its volatility, yet allows you to continue to grow your net worth.

The "Later" Bucket: Now that you are covered for the more immediate future by the "Now" and "Soon" buckets, these monies are designed for long-term growth and legacy planning. This is particularly important when thinking of providing for a spouse's future income upon the death of the first.[23]

I would highly recommend this book to you and your financial advisor. Smith covers all the bases, which can be adjusted for your individual lifestyle and goals.

. . .

WHAT QUALIFIED PLAN IS BEST FOR YOU?

You may be approaching that age when your company policy mandates retirement. Or you may have been laid off or lost your business during the pandemic lockdown. Or perhaps you have made a conscious decision to invest your remaining years in a civic outreach or ministry. In any case, you will need funds to support yourself and your family.

As we have pointed out, most people spend more time planning their next vacation than their retirement years, let alone their eternal destiny after this life! But if you are among the lucky ones—an employee whose company offered a retirement package, for example—you have something saved up. If not, as we have mentioned, it is not too late to begin investing now. And the best qualified retirement plan is the one that mitigates your particular situation.

401(K)

"A 401k is an employer-sponsored retirement account. It allows an employee to dedicate a percentage of their pre-tax salary to a retirement account. These funds are invested in a range of vehicles like stocks, bonds, mutual funds, and cash."[24]

Simply put, if you were employed by a company that subscribed to this plan for their employees as a hiring incentive, you probably agreed to a specific percentage of your paycheck to be directed to the 401(k) account by your employer, the investments (stocks, bonds, mutual funds, ETFs) selected by you. There are many benefits to this plan:

- **Tax-deferred:** Monies accumulate, tax-deferred, until withdrawn at retirement. (As of the writing of this book, there is a penalty of 10% for early withdrawal, usually before age 59½, with some exceptions provided under the CARES Act passed during the pandemic. If you did not withdraw early, you will receive the entire amount upon retirement.) Taxes are paid only on the amount withdrawn (required minimum distribution) with the exception of those who have a Roth IRA/401(k).

- **Employer-matched:** Most employers will match your contribution up to a certain dollar or percentage amount, which means "free money" for you! Therefore, hopefully you put as much money as possible into your 401(k) plan allowed by your budget.
- **Not a Savings Account:** Remember, this is primarily a retirement account, not to be used for your new large-screen TV or your new car. There is a provision in some 401(k) plans that allow you to access your monies for emergencies without penalty, via a loan provision that can be repaid through payroll deductions.
- **Creditor-sheltered:** This investment plan is protected under ERISA (Employee Retirement Income Security Act), so in the event of a financial downturn or personal crisis, such as a medical emergency, your creditors cannot garnish this fund unless you haven't paid your taxes. This is the major difference between a 401(k) plan, defined benefit plan, qualified profit-sharing plan, and an IRA account. Check your state guidelines.
- **Wealth-building:** As your investment grows, so does your net worth!

IRA (INDIVIDUAL RETIREMENT ACCOUNT)

If you are a retiree, an independent contractor, or simply want to invest more than a 401(k) will allow, this is the plan for you. The process is the same: You will simply do the investing yourself—preferably with the aid of your financial advisor(s).

ROTH IRA

If you make under a certain amount of money per year, single or married, you will probably want to consider this option. Unlike the traditional IRA, contributions to the Roth are not tax-deductible, but earnings grow tax-free. Withdrawals are also tax-free. The future of the Roth IRA/401(k) option is uncertain.

IF YOU NEED CASH NOW...

In this post-pandemic era, many people are temporarily out of work or struggling with the new reality that their old job may never reappear. While we believe that the economy will turn around in time, many people are faced with a cash crunch in the meantime.

I agree with the findings of a writer for the periodical *Journal Reports,* Cheryl Winoker Munk, who gives ten suggested sources for income for the short term, both pros and cons:

- **Borrow from family:** If your family is financially secure, this may be the best option. No credit check. No interest. Flexible repayment plan. But family should not become your bank, although loans of any size might be considered an "upfront inheritance."
- **Short-term savings accounts:** This seems a likely source of income for the present. Bank savings accounts. Money market accounts. CDs. But there may be penalties for early withdrawals in some cases.
- **"529" plans:** This is an education savings plan. For those with this long-term strategy in place for their children or

future children, drawing on this account makes sense as it is somewhat easy to replace it later with loans, grants, and scholarships.

- **Retirement accounts:** This seems the most logical since retirement may be in the distant future. But remember, early withdrawal incurs penalties and taxes. And 401(k) loans have rigid repayment schedules. I do not recommend this as a first resort as failure to repay means you will not have the funds needed when you do reach retirement.

- **Annuities:** You may be able to receive a partial withdrawal without penalty. But there will be an IRS penalty for those annuitants younger than 59½.

- **Life insurance policies:** Withdrawals are possible, but these may be taxed as ordinary income. Also, there may be limits on how much may be repaid in a year and surrender charges may apply.

- **Home-equity line of credit or loan**—With low interest rates, the option to withdraw money as needed, and a lengthy repayment schedule, a line of credit loan may be appealing. But remember, a home-equity loan is a one-time lump sum with a fixed interest rate.

- **Credit card:** While this option seems favorable since some people use credit cards so freely, don't forget the high interest rates. On the other hand, if you're really in a hole financially, you might be able to negotiate with the credit card company for grace later.

- **Margin loans:** If you are a shareholder with margin loans, you might be able to borrow against their value. But if the value of your holdings falls below a certain level, you will have to deposit more cash, or your broker will have to liquidate some securities.

- **Social Security:** At full retirement age, you can request a lump-sum distribution for up to six months of payments. The downside: if you are expecting to live a long life, you will receive lower payments later.[25]

WHICH STORY ENDING WILL YOU WRITE?

So, let's wrap this up. Take a look at the three scenarios mentioned and see if you can glean some important principles/warnings for your own future:

SCENARIO #1: You have reached the age of retirement and have achieved your goal of a million dollars between your own and your spouse's IRA accounts. You are completely out of debt and are ready to relax and enjoy life. In a meeting with your financial advisor, he or she gives you the following review of your financial standing, along with an accurate picture of your present physical and emotional status:

- IRA accounts will provide you $40,000–50,000 per year.
- Social Security will provide $36,000 per year.
- Rental income from your properties in your LLC— $5,000 per month net of expenses on average.
- Both you and your wife have excellent health.
- You have two children and six grandchildren living in two different states.
- You are 66½ and your wife is 62.

Now, with time on your hands, you get up in the mornings and go to the local restaurant for breakfast with friends. You shoot the breeze, rehashing old stories and talk a little politics and the weather. Occasionally, one of your buddies will discuss some past engineering feat or you will mention some successful business innovation you have scored during your career.

Meanwhile, your wife is home, drinking her morning coffee and watching her favorite newscast. Three mornings a week, she takes a Zumba class at the local health spa, then goes to help out at a food pantry. She also teaches Sunday school at your church, volunteers as a tutor at the elementary school when needed and has lunch with friends at least once a week. In the evenings, she keeps up with the grandchildren via Zoom calls.

After breakfast with the guys, you come home to a few odd chores on your wife's to-do list, then eat lunch and take a nap. Around 2 p.m., you go outside and hit a golf ball around the backyard in preparation for your weekly golf game—your only form of exercise.

One year after you retire, you begin having some memory problems and, shortly thereafter, are diagnosed with dementia. No more golf or breakfast with your buddies since you are losing recall of which club to swing when, not to mention the names of your friends. Two years later, you have developed full-fledged Alzheimer's.

Your wife must decide whether to hire a full-time nurse to help with your care because she can no longer physically handle your deteriorating health. Soon, she makes the tough decision to put you in the memory care division of a local nursing home.

Fortunately, your financial advisor had urged you to purchase a long-term care insurance policy since neither you nor your spouse had received a pension from your workplace. Your wife sells the rental properties, which she can no longer manage by herself. She then invests the monies in a diversified stock portfolio to provide more income, which she gives to the two children, using the $15,000 gift exemption.

Shortly afterward, you pass away, and your wife sells the house and moves to North Carolina to be near her daughter and the grandchildren. She misses you, of course, and is grieving the lost time that you could have spent together in the years you had prepared to enjoy. Still, she is happy that you are now in heaven, fully healed and enjoying the rich rewards of your eternal inheritance.

SCENARIO #2: Let's change this story a bit to achieve a little different ending. Same financial/physical profile. In this scene, you only eat breakfast with your friends a couple of mornings a week, but exercise three mornings a week at the Y. You have a part-time job as a landscaper at the gardening center, where you create additional income by engaging in one of the hobbies you enjoy most. On off days, you help your wife at the food pantry and, on Sundays, lead a mentoring group for younger men at your church.

At age 75, with no signs of dementia or Alzheimer's, you sell your rental properties and invest in more liquid stocks, giving each child the $15,000 gift exemption, but leaving plenty in the investment to draw a return well into old age!

SCENARIO #3: To our national shame, many Americans fall into a category where the couple has worked in various jobs, and they are now divorced and their nasty separations have swallowed up most of their retirement monies. The husband has a small pension of $250 from the years he worked for the city. As a former waitress at a local restaurant, the wife has no retirement funds.

At ages 67 and 64 respectively, they decide to retire and live off their Social Security. He receives $1,800 per month, and her benefit is only half that amount, with a total monthly income of $2,700 per month.

They still owe the balance on their small house—about $25,000—with a mortgage payment of $440 per month. They have never invested in the stock market because they considered it too risky and never trusted their employers to execute a 401(k) plan for them. Therefore, they have been able to save only $6,000 to see them through their remaining years. With credit card debt totaling $15,000, once they pay all their monthly bills, including a car payment, there will be nothing to leave for their children.

Sad to say, this is the story for over 30% of all Americans after working for over 40 years. If you don't want this to be your epitaph, you need to make some substantial changes to your lifestyle, including saving for the future—if not for your own future, then for the future of those who come after you.

The last scenario illustrates the proverb: *"Go ahead—be lazy and passive. But you'll go hungry if you live that way"* (Proverbs 19:15 TPT). The second points out the scientific premise that the brain is a muscle; when it remains inactive, the idleness leads to atrophy of the mind just like any other muscle. Staying involved keeps you mentally alert and physically sound.

You definitely don't want to wind up in the third category. If you rely on the principles taught in God's Word and the advice of financial counselors, you can continue to contribute to society in ways that are meaningful to you and glorifying to God.

Bottom Line: *Most people spend more time planning their next vacation than their retirement years. I hope you are among those who have invested wisely and have something saved up. If not, it is not too late to begin investing now!*

Chapter 8

LEAVING A LEGACY

The happiest people I know are those who give
their money away.
  —S. Truett Cathy Founder, *Chick-fil-A*

I HAVE SPENT the last seven chapters laying out a road map for
to how to build your net worth. In the next several pages, I want
to help you understand how to let it go.

One of the great advantages of building a substantial net worth
is being able to help people when they are in need. For example,
when my oldest son was a senior in high school, we were able to
offer his friend Jason a safe harbor when he ran into some difficulties in his own household.

One day, while Jason was living with us, I noticed an ad by
a local insurance company that was going out of business and
selling all of their office equipment. So, I took the boys to the sale
and bought them several older personal computers. When we got
home, my wife nearly had a stroke when we unloaded our purchases.

The basement of our home (vintage 1860s) was like a dungeon—sandstone walls and dirt floor. We had dug out the floor and poured concrete but left the sandstone walls intact. It was the perfect space for our boys and their friends to use their imagination and skills and come up with innovative ideas. And that is just what my son and Jason did. In no time, they took apart several of the old computers and tinkered with them to assemble another computer.

Today, many years later, Jason runs his own computer service company, Sentec Systems. Our comfortable net worth at that time enabled us to help Jason when he most needed it. Now, as a business owner, he is well on his way to building his own net worth, ending his family's cycle of financial and spiritual poverty. He still calls my wife "Mom" and me "Dad."

YOU CAN'T TAKE IT WITH YOU

The story I have just shared with you is only one of many scenarios that are possible when one faithfully invests in stocks, bonds, and other options that provide a return on the investment. It is only when you have accumulated some measure of financial success that you are able to not only provide for your own family but also share with others who cannot provide for themselves.

Listen to these testimonies from some well-known philanthropists and one tiny nun from Italy. Truett Cathy famously said, "Wealth is worth it only when you give it away."[26] Warren Buffett, one of the two wealthiest men in America, said, "I have arranged that all of the money—and it will be 99 percent of what I earned—will be distributed, at the latest, ten years after my estate is settled."[27] But it was Mother Teresa who got to the heart of the matter when she said, "Let us not be satisfied with just giving money. Money is not enough. Money can be got, but they need your hearts to love them. So, spread your love everywhere you go."[28] Whatever you have of this world's goods and/or the money you have invested, I hope you do realize the importance of *giving* while you are still *living.*

If you have children, you have likely considered the fact that you will not always be around to step in with a little extra cash if they occasionally hit a time when there is more month than money. And, of course, you will want to leave behind the funds to provide for your spouse in the event that you pre-decease him/her.

What good husband doesn't want to leave his wife ample provision for the rest of her life? What good parent doesn't want their children to be better off financially than they were? And leaving something of monetary value to your descendants is altogether biblical: *"A good man leaves an inheritance for his children's children"* (Proverbs 22:3).

• • •

Recently, an older couple (in their eighties) was in my office, concerned that their investments were not performing well, and they were in real danger of exhausting all their savings and investments before their lives ended.

We spent a good hour reviewing their situation. Several years earlier, this couple had begun with an investment of $150,000. Now there was only $40,000 left. After asking a few more questions, it was pretty obvious that they had made—and were continuing to make—several mistakes:

- They had no clue as to what they were paying in fees to their investment firm.
- They had withdrawn too much money—10% to 15%—from their account. (Our rule is to take no more than 5% per year if you want your monies to outlast you!)

- They were giving away too much money to questionable charitable institutions.
- They had made some poor investment choices along the way.

I don't use flowery language or a bunch of empty words to appease my clients—or in this case, my *potential* clients. In fact, I talked straight, asking them if they were willing to reduce their withdrawals to no more than 5% each year. During our conversation, I had learned that they had been scammed out of some of their monies over the past several years. As a result, this couple was in danger of outliving their money.

Even though I did my best to spell out the consequences of failing to follow sound advice, they refused. You can lead a horse to water, but you can't make him drink.

PROTECTING YOUR ASSETS
Annuities and Life Insurance

Annuities are the most confusing financial product available to the consuming public. There are almost as many types of annuities as there are languages—and they are almost as difficult to understand.

Basically, an annuity is a life insurance product that gives you either simple or compounded interest, usually guaranteed by the full faith and credit of the insurance company. Consequently, the annuity is only as good as the insurance company's financial well-being. These insurance companies invest your monies in bonds, real estate, and some equities, then take 1% to 3% in fees and expenses before paying you the difference. Therefore, they take all of the risk to give you a fixed rate of return, which is why they are so expensive.

Annuities do have a place in some people's portfolios. Let me give you a couple of examples:

1. Those who do not qualify for life insurance: Suppose you want to leave a certain amount to a loved one or charity upon your death, but for health reasons, you have been unable to get life insurance. You can, however, invest in a variable annuity or fixed annuity with a guaranteed death benefit that compounds in interest. Remember that annuities are taxable to the person or entity receiving the death benefit. The taxable amount is the earnings that have accumulated, tax-deferred, over the annuitant's lifetime.

2. Those who are afraid of taking a risk: Some of the people who come to me for financial advice just can't—or don't want to—understand stocks and the way they work. Or they simply refuse to take a risk. When I ask my usual question: "How much money do you need to keep in the bank so you can sleep at night?", the answer is almost always, "One hundred percent of it!" I have tried to educate these people on the power of equity investing. Shown them the hypothetical illustration of how much they can increase their earnings. Suggested books to read, proving that equity investing will help them grow their net worth. Yet, they panic every time the stock market takes a dip!

For these people, the only two investment options are CDs or annuities. In this low-interest-rate environment, you would be lucky to make 3% on your investment since these products earn only simple or compound interest. In other words, in the case of simple interest, $100,000 makes you $3,000 per year. Since the interest is not compounded, this means that next year, your $103,000 would still only give you an additional $3,000.

In view of these facts, I strongly suggest the following:

- **Avoid** simple interest contracts.
- **Avoid** indexed annuities.
- **Avoid** annuitizing an annuity. If you should stumble into this option, here is what happens: Your contract will pay you a fixed monthly income based on your age, sex, and underlying investment earnings of the life insurance company for ten years. Once the ten years is up—and if you, the annuitant, should die—your heirs receive $0! Not only that, but anything can happen to the insurance company during those ten years. Check out the fiasco of AIG in 2008–2009 and Mutual Benefit Life in the '80s.

Variable Annuities: Contracts in which the contract owner/annuitant shares in the investment risks with the insurance company. You may pick other mutual funds or ETFs to invest in within the parameters of the contract.

Fixed Annuities: Contracts in which the annuitant is given a guaranteed rate of return for a certain period of time. As of this writing, that guaranteed rate would be 2% to 3%, depending upon the length of the contract—usually three to seven years. In this case, the life insurance company assumes 100% of the risk.

Indexed Annuities: Contracts that pay an interest rate based on the performance of a specified market index. To be avoided if possible!

LIFE INSURANCE: HOW MUCH IS YOUR LIFE WORTH

Isn't it interesting that we insure almost everything we buy—cars, houses, boats, tractors—but we don't always insure the people who drive the cars, live in the house, use the stuff, etc.? Without *you,* the "stuff" is worthless. Still, when it is time to think about your financial legacy, it is wise to consider the projected needs of those you leave behind.

So, who needs life insurance and what type?

Term Life Insurance: Best described by its own terms. It lasts for a specific period of time—in other words, a term: ten, twenty, or thirty years. In some cases, you could extend that period of time for a substantial increase in premium per year. Term insurance is very inexpensive because few people ever have a claim due to the policies lapsing before they are 70 or 80 years old. In today's world, there is a new type of term insurance that is a hybrid of universal life and term insurance that I call "term for life." It has a guaranteed no-lapse provision if you pay the premium up to age 100. This policy has no cash value accumulation, unlike universal life and whole life.

Universal Life Insurance: A form of whole life insurance that has a cost tied to the growth of the cash value minus the death benefit, called Net Amount at Risk. As your cash value grows, the cost of the insurance decreases. The two kinds of universal life are fixed and variable. The fixed—the insurance company takes all the risk. The variable—you, the consumer, assume the risk, but you also have the opportunity of a greater reward.

Traditional Whole Life Insurance: Has a guarantee backed by the full faith and credit of the insurance company. This form of insurance has a guaranteed fixed premium for life to age 95 or 100. Unlike term insurance that expires after a certain period of time, this form of life insurance will provide you with permanent insurance for as long as the average person lives. Most whole life insurance companies also return a portion of your premium to you after a certain number of years, an amount that you could use to either reduce your premium or to purchase more life insurance. If your current financial advisor isn't life insurance-licensed, you may have to add a life insurance agent to your advisory team.

So, let's make it simple: If your life insurance needs are permanent, longer than thirty years, you might need universal life or whole life. If you're buying life insurance to pay off your mortgage or debt or replace the primary spouse's income, then you would probably need term insurance. In other words, if you have a temporary problem, term insurance. If you have a permanent need (i.e., stock redemption agreements or federal estate taxes to pay), you will need whole life.

- **For those under age 60:** If you are married and have young children, children in college, a mortgage, and other debt, you will need a policy insuring your life for ten times your annual income.
- **For business owners:** You may need to take out life insurance policies on key personnel and for stock redemption agreements. In other words, if you are in business with a partner and your partner dies, life insurance provides the monies to buy your partner's percentage of the business from his widow. Or to provide the necessary capital if needed to hire a replacement. In this particular instance, you may need whole life insurance versus term insurance. You will need an additional life insurance policy on yourself of one to two times the value of your business.
- **For wealthy persons who have accumulated more than $24 million in assets or what is commonly referred to as the estate tax exemption.** (Under the proposed new tax law, this amount might be reduced to $7.5 million— the estate tax exemption limit.) The tax on assets above

that amount is 40% to 50%, depending upon your state of residence. One of the best ways to pay that tax is via life insurance owned by an irrevocable life insurance trust. Obviously, some careful planning needs to be executed.

Especially in light of COVID-19, I make these points in great detail, having seen too many cases where families and business owners are not prepared for the unexpected.

YOUR TRUE NET WORTH

Throughout this book, you have read the term *net worth* many times. But you might have noticed that this subtitle added a third word—*true.* In other words, the value of a life cannot be calculated in dollars and cents. Take the Proverbs 31 woman, for example: *"Her worth is far above rubies"* (v. 10). This proverb goes on to list all the ways in which this virtuous woman serves and blesses her husband, her family, her helpers, and the poor. She serves as an example to all women.

I began this chapter with a story about my oldest son and his young friend Jason, who had some serious difficulties and needed a place to stay for a while. My heart went out to Jason, and because we were in a position to help him, both financially and spiritually, my wife and I took him in, hoping to give him some love and guidance during a traumatic time in his life.

Because we have continued to put money in its proper place—saving, investing for the long run, and sharing—we have been able to reach out to help others through the years.

• • •

By the time my business had been up and running for a while, and I felt secure about leaving things in the capable hands of my associates, I joined a group from our church making a trip to the city of Kitali, Kenya, in northwest Africa. Our purpose was to investigate the possibility of supporting an orphanage and school in that region.

When we arrived, I told my pastor friend, Bill, that I wanted to walk around the town to get a feel for the area and maybe talk with some shop owners. To my surprise, I found that not a single shop owner was African, but Indian—descendants of people who were brought over from India to build railroads when both Kenya and India were British colonies. Meanwhile, the native African males were hired as cheap field labor by U.N. "overseers," turning the wheat and grain into liquor while their children starved. Apparently, not much has changed since those early years.

The land surrounding Kitali was rich and fertile—some of the best in Kenya—and, as a farm boy myself, I saw the great potential to improve the lives of the poor Africans. I saw the men using ancient plows driven by oxen and thought of the modern farm implements that could make their work easier. I saw the plight of the women who were treated as property, useful only for producing more children to work the fields and thought of the freedom they could enjoy in Christ, who has created all people equal in His sight.

We returned home with somewhat heavy hearts, but I was determined to help my new Kenyan friends reverse their course of poverty. In the next few months, some of my clients and I were able to raise over $40,000 to take back to Africa. With this seed money, we started four businesses that I felt confident would be successful based on the observations I had made on our first trip.

On the second trip, as the old saying goes, we didn't just hand them a fish, we taught them *how* to fish!

• • •

Another example was a widow who came to me for counsel. Typical of many families, she and her husband had always lived paycheck to paycheck. Her late husband had tried to break the cycle by investing in various schemes and gadgets, none of which had come to fruition. The wife, a church secretary, barely made enough to cover the monthly bills.

With her husband's unexpected death and with no savings, she was in danger of losing her house to the bank. I learned of her plight from my wife, who was her good friend, and together we decided to help.

God has given me a deep concern for widows and orphans. The first deacons in the early Church were appointed to care for them, and this is exactly what I decided to do.

After making an appointment with the bank holding the mortgage, I purchased the house. The woman and I agreed that she would pay some rent and eventually repossess the house from me when she and her sons could afford it.

A few years later, the youngest son bought the house from me at cost. A sad story with a happier ending because we had the financial (and spiritual) net worth to share with a sister in Christ.

You can do it too. If you will put into practice the simple steps I have given you in this book and follow the teachings of God's Word—the best Guidebook ever written for successful living—you can build *true* net worth!

Bottom Line: *Many Christians have listened to the wrong people and have let their emotions determine their investments and lifestyle choices. They ensure their stuff but don't ensure the people who drive and own and clean the stuff. Therefore, the price of insecurity, fear, and all the what-ifs could rob you of the money or the assets to help the orphan and the widow, thus helping to build your* true *net worth.*

Chapter 9

WHAT'S NEXT?

Behold, I am coming soon! My reward is with me,
and I will give to everyone according to what he has done.
(Revelation 22:12)

IF YOU HAVE never read the end of the Good Book, now might
be a good time. The Bible is essentially the history of the Jewish people, prophesying the birth, life, death, and resurrection
of Jesus Christ, the Son of God, in the Old Testament, and the
fulfillment of those prophecies in the New Testament. That's
definitely Good News! But this sacred Book, the bestseller of all
time, also gives us some insight into what the future holds for us
twenty-first-century dwellers.

Have you ever wondered: Why the Jews? Why were they en-
slaved by the Egyptians for four hundred years? Why were they
assaulted and their population decimated by the Persian Empire
after ruling the Middle East for several years? Why were they

captured again by the Roman Empire and then the Ottoman Empire, finally dispersed around the globe, and persecuted everywhere they went?

Somehow, though, the Jewish people were able to acquire great wealth, even helping to finance the Revolutionary War through Haymaker Solomon, an immigrant from Poland, before suffering the Holocaust two hundred years later, when 6 million of them were slaughtered by Hitler's Nazi regime. How has the smallest democracy in the world survived all those ancient atrocities, only to go to war again in 1948, 1967, and 1973 with their Arab neighbors, who continue to plague this tiny nation with ongoing terrorist attacks?

You may say they have survived because of the continued financial and military support of America. Only partly true. There is a greater reason: God's plan for Israel to be a light to the nations—and His purpose that those who bless Israel will be blessed (see Genesis 12:2–3).

So, what has all this to do with your net worth? Probably more than you realize...

MY PERSONAL PREDICTION

Because of the situation in which we find ourselves today—depending upon which media source you are listening to—you could either believe that we are facing another Great Depression or an economic utopia. Neither of these extremes is accurate. The truth is somewhere in between. Let me offer my observations.

First, from a spiritual perspective: When our 45th president made the announcement in December of 2017 that he was moving the U.S. Embassy from Tel Aviv to Jerusalem, which was then declared the official capital of Israel, I knew that God would keep His promise to bless America. The naysayers began their diatribe, of course, spouting off that the Muslim world would surely retaliate and there would be all-out war. Didn't happen. What did happen was that more Arab nations are recognizing Israel's existence and want peace, beginning with the United Arab Emirates and Sudan. More are slated to follow.

Second, from a secular perspective: We no longer need Arab oil to operate our economy. We are energy independent. Think about it. What led to the long recession of the 1970s? Energy prices skyrocketed because we were dependent on our enemies for oil. The government enacted the fifty-five-mile-per-hour speed limits and other energy-saving regulations and wage and price controls, concerned that we would be out of oil by 2020! Not only that, but we lost our manufacturing base due to high energy/labor costs. All that has changed over the past ten years, with fracking, wind, solar, and enough natural gas for at least two hundred years. The United States is now a net exporter of liquified natural gas, oil, and distillates. Plus, we lead in the manufacture of technology services—Microsoft, Apple, Tesla, Amazon, Google, Zoom, etc.—all based here in the United States. No wonder China wants to steal our intellectual property!

And that's not all! What about agriculture? Interestingly, agriculture plays more of a role in basic economics than you might know. Up through the Great Depression, agriculture was responsible for 70% of the U.S. economy. Now it is less than 5.5% of our total economic gross domestic product (GDP). No government can grow their economy without a self-sustaining food source. Throughout history, starving people are one of the ingredients of the prime recipe for a revolution. Just a few months ago, the media spun an over-sensationalized story that launched a run on meat because of the temporary closure of a large meat-packing plant, owned by a Chinese conglomerate, due to COVID-19.

But imagine how much more desperate the situation is in India and China. Lest you believe some of the forecasts that predict China will become the world's super-power, you might want to

Google their ability to feed themselves, not to mention their lack of water. With 20% of the world's population, China has only 6% of the world's water supply—and that is badly polluted—whereas we in the United States have 21% of the world's fresh water in the Great Lakes alone!

So, be encouraged! America is agriculturally and energy independent—two key ingredients to a growing economy.

"But what about the grim warnings coming from the progressive Left?" you may ask. Of course, we are to be aware of global events that can have a dramatic influence on where and what to invest in. And the pandemic of 2020 will continue to have its fallout, but it may also provide unprecedented opportunities for investment.

In 2001, the market went down substantially. Many investors sold their stocks and bonds and have yet to get back into the market. Many others sold out after the downturn of 2008–2009 and have not reinvested. More recently, because of the COVID pandemic, others sold out in April and May of 2020 and are earning a whopping 0.05% on their savings.

Let's look at the three indices in 2000, as well as 2009, 2015, and 2020. (See Chart 4 at the back of this book.)

My question to you is this: Are you worth more today than you were five years ago? Or ten years ago? If not, why not? (If you're worth less than you were five or ten years ago, you need to make a change. You need to start an action plan, suggestions for which you will find in the workbook that accompanies this book.)

WILL THE DOLLAR MAKE IT?

Until the biggest commodities in the world—oil, coffee, sugar, natural gas, corn, wheat, soybeans—are NOT traded in dollars, I am not worried about the value of the dollar. And watch out for those peddling gold and silver. If they are counting on the dollar to drop to $0, the cows in my pasture would be worth more than their gold or silver. At least, in the worst-case scenario, I could milk my cows, make cheese, or, as a last resort, eat them. You can't eat gold bricks or coins or your grandmother's silver tea service. If things get that bad, what earthly product could save you?

I am not suggesting you should not own some gold or silver, just not in your IRA. But I *am* concerned about Bitcoin and other non-regulated cryptocurrencies.[1] Many financial "prophets" have predicted the fall of the dollar and the rise of some other form of global currency, such as digital currency. In talking to very intelligent people in the field, not one has been able to explain how this works, its underlying value, or what really makes it worth serious investment.

My fear is that since cryptocurrency is non-regulated, it is a prime target for terrorist groups and other unscrupulous organizations who want to avoid regulations. Plus—and this is vitally important—any investment in Bitcoin or other forms of cryptocurrency is high-risk!

My rule of thumb: If you can't understand it, don't invest in it!

THE BOTTOM LINE

For the past eight chapters, I have attempted to leave you with a little wisdom I have gleaned from my years of experience in the area of finance and some practical procedures for building your net worth—both spiritually and financially—and ensuring your legacy to future generations. Here is a recap:

1. Whatever your age, if you are still holding onto bitterness, hurt, and unforgiveness toward someone, how will you

---

1 See https://cointelegraph.com/explained.

ever build true net worth? So, take some time out to consider what is really important. It's your life! It's your money! It's your opportunity!

2. The greatest asset in any business is people—your staff, your associates, your clients. These are the multipliers that will ensure growth and will help you increase the value of your enterprise.

3. Investing in the stock market is investing in the world— the companies founded by hard-working people who produce the goods and services that fuel our global economy (i.e., the capitalistic way).

4. *After you have considered each of the investment options available to you, it is wise to invest in a variety of asset classes (i.e., healthcare, transportation, real estate, etc.); in other words, diversify. A well-rounded portfolio will give you insurance against the probability of market fluctuations. And be sure to rebalance annually with your financial team.*

5. *Once too much bad debt sucks you in, you're in quicksand unless someone throws you a lifeline. As one investment expert warned, "People don't plan to fail, they fail to plan."*

6. *By using your God-given gifts and talents, along with humility, passion, dedication, and teamwork, you can build a successful business. But don't forget to create a succession plan that will allow the business to continue to succeed after your passing.*

7. Most people spend more time planning their next vacation than their retirement years. I hope you are among those who have invested wisely and have something saved up. If not, it is not too late to begin investing now!

8. I pray that my story and a few practical tips will give you closure to your pain and suffering so that the forces of spiritual and financial poverty will never be a part of your legacy.

9. Some people are expecting their reward only in heaven; therefore, they do not prepare for success on earth. Don't be one of them.

10. Be open to hear, see, and discern the truth because the truth will set you free. Free from fear! Free from failure! Free from futility!

HOW TO SURVIVE IN THE POST-PANDEMIC ERA

Down through the ages, few societies have enjoyed the enormous success brought about by our Constitution and Bill of Rights, with the rule of law, clearly explained by Milton Friedman: "Because we live in a largely free society, we tend to forget how limited is the span of time and the part of the globe for which there has ever been anything like political freedom: the typical state of mankind is tyranny, servitude, and misery. The nineteenth century and early twentieth century in the Western world stand out as striking exceptions. Political freedom in this instance clearly came along with the free market and the development of capitalist institutions."[29]

When a college dropout like Bill Gates[2] can create a mega-company from his garage, or Steve Jobs can develop a company called Apple, which could be the first to reach a valuation of over $2 trillion, or even a farm boy like myself can multiply a company by twenty times in an economically depressed area, you know that America is a nation that still offers the freedom to work hard and realize our dreams.

As we have stated previously, we are in danger of losing our freedom to prosper and to pursue our very way of life. Sure, we need to rectify mistakes of the past, humble ourselves and ask

---

2 Because of his brilliant innovative ideas, Bill Gates has received at least seven honorary degrees from various institutions of higher learning, including an honorary doctorate from his alma mater, Harvard, thirty years after he dropped out following his sophomore year.

God to forgive sins of racial prejudice, abortion, and failure to do justly in our daily commerce. The lines between right and wrong, good and evil have never been more clearly drawn, and not everyone is on board with doing good in our divisive culture.

Here are a few suggestions for navigating this difficult time from the Source of all financial and spiritual wealth, the Bible:

Control Your Own Anger: With racism and politics being the driving force today, the spirit of anger has been unleashed around the world.[3] We have actually witnessed grown people breaking out in fistfights at their kids' soccer games. Not to mention the violent groups—"peaceful protestors"—storming city streets, looting, burning buildings, and attacking innocent citizens, including elderly people on their walkers! It appears that many have lost all sense of the value of property, even the value of life itself. Jesus Himself warned about this centuries ago: *"Many will be offended, will betray one another, and will hate one another...and because lawlessness will abound, the love of many will grow cold. But he who endures to the end will be saved"* (Matthew 24:10–12).

There has never been so much visible hatred in this country. I have even heard some say that they hate one of our recent presidents. I don't hate him, although he cost me 50% of our business—health insurance and 401(k). It would be easy to seethe with anger and seek vengeance. But the spirit of negativity is like quicksand. I don't intend to give the Enemy (the devil, not flesh and blood) any ground.

I may have lost a few possessions and some business, but I am encouraged to "endure to the end." The word *endure* is huge. It means "to hold one's ground in conflict, bear up against adversity, hold out under stress, stand firm, persevere under pressure, wait calmly and courageously."[30] Try this when everything

---

3 In this context, I highly recommend the book *Blackout* by Candace Owens.

else—business, sales, income, health—goes south.

Choose Friends and Business Associates Wisely: Two thousand years ago, during a politically volatile time when Rome was ruling the Middle East, Jesus was having a meal with twelve men in an Upper Room in Jerusalem. He looked around the table at each of them. These men had walked with Him for three years, had heard His teachings, had seen His miracles, and had become His intimate friends. But this very night, one of them would betray Him—for money! Thirty pieces of silver, which by today's measure would amount to between $90 to $3,000![31]

In the midst of conflict and confusion, choose your friends and associates wisely. You need to know who will stand with you and who would be willing to sell you out.

I have been stabbed in the back by some within my own industry. When a disagreement arises, they have chosen the "thirty pieces of silver" over loyalty to a friend. The Bible says, *"The love of money is the root of all kinds of evil"* (1 Timothy 6:10). On the other hand, a good friend of mine paraphrased it this way: "The wise use of money is the root of all good."

Don't Let Your Emotions Control Your Investment Decisions: I wish I had gotten a second degree from Otterbein University—one in Psychology. I tend to spend more time controlling people's emotions than managing their portfolios/retirement plans, especially in times like these. With twenty-four-hour news—mostly negative or sensationalized—and even Christian writers playing on our fears, it is very difficult to keep people invested in the stock market and not let fear drive their decision. With fear being such a strong emotion, very few stay invested throughout their lifetime, or they try to define the market for themselves and decide they know when to sell and when to buy. Chart 5 at the back of this book illustrates that it seldom matters who is in the

White House—Democrat or Republican—or even who is holding seats in Congress.

FAIL YOUR WAY TO SUCCESS

As we wind down, I dare you to try to match my list of failures—both personally and professionally. You have read about my lack of confidence as a novice schoolteacher. Then there was my inability to multi-task when I was attempting to learn the insurance business while farming. But that isn't all. Remember my stuttering problem and my long-term feud with my dad? All of these failed challenges could have spelled utter despair and defeat. But I didn't give up...and I wasn't alone.

If Thomas Edison had stopped with one or two experiments, we would not have the incandescent lightbulb. If Jonas Salk had given up on his medical project, he would not have developed a vaccine for polio. If I had put off forgiving my father, I might never have stopped stuttering and would likely not be where I am today.

I have decided that I will not let the "ifs" of life determine my course of action. I will press on, no matter what the stock market says. I will give it my best shot for my clients every day. I will never give up!

NO MORE SHUTDOWNS

Our pastor, Micah Pelkey, has been teaching a series of sermons on the word *open*. I imagine he was inspired by the fact that so many churches, schools, and businesses have been closed during the COVID-19 pandemic.

Open. I like the concept. *Open* to change. *Open* to new ideas. *Open* to breaking destructive cycles—like financial and spiritual poverty.

If you are resisting change in this new reality, I ask you to consider praying this prayer:

> I pray...that the God of our Lord Jesus Christ, the Father of glory, may give to [me] the spirit of wisdom and revelation in the knowledge of Him, the eyes of [my] understanding being enlightened, that [I] may know what is the hope of His calling, what are the riches of the glory of His inheritance in the saints, and what is the exceeding greatness of His power toward us who believe. (Ephesians 1:17–19)

Pray that the eyes of your heart may be open and that you will be willing to change your thinking about investing in stocks. That you will change your mind about spending more than you make and living paycheck to paycheck. I personally pray that, when you reach age 70, you will not be living on Social Security and some government handout only. There is a better way.

And when you come to the end of your days on earth, may you have stored up in heaven treasures of faith, forgiveness, hope, and love. You will have all of eternity to spend the riches of His glory!

Bottom Line: *Some people are expecting their reward only in heaven; therefore, they do not prepare for success on earth. Don't be one of them.*

Chapter 10

EXPECT THE UNEXPECTED!

My soul, wait silently for God alone,
for my expectation is from Him.
(Psalm 62:5)

RECENTLY, I WAS attending a special church conference where a Messianic rabbi was giving his perspective on current and possible future events. One phrase struck me like lightning: "Expect the unexpected!" Only days later, I came down with the COVID-19 virus! Two weeks shy of my 65th birthday. And only a couple of months after the unexpected passing of my brother Lyle. God has a way of getting our attention, doesn't He?

While in quarantine, when I was able to spend more time at home in prayer and talking with my ghostwriter and my friend, Mickey Robinson, I realized I needed to give you more. Let's call it a "game plan."

Over the weekend, I watched the Masters golf tournament. Almost every player, before his next shot—especially the approach shot to the green—gets out a little black book that he and his caddy have compiled. They look at the pin placement, the slope of the green, the velocity of the wind (if any), and the lie of the ball. One quarter of an inch can determine whether you can make a birdie putt, land in the sand trap, or roll off the green entirely! Usually, the player who wins the tournament has hit the most fairways and greens in regulation. That was true of this year's winner—Dustin Johnson. No penalty shots and the most greens and fairways, as well as record low scores. Great job, Dustin!

With the new equipment and technology, the game of golf has been refined to a quarter of an inch. The operative word is *detail*.

All successful coaches pay attention to detail. Football coaches watch game film of upcoming opponents to find the team's weaknesses and strengths. In this way, they can prepare their own players and put together a game plan that will lead them to victory. In a football game, you will see the coaches with a play chart in their hands, compiled during the week with their staff and players. This chart contains plays that they think they can execute to exploit the other team's weaknesses.

For example, if the coach has little data on an opposing defensive back—say he is a rookie player—that coach may target this player with a certain pass play. Why? To test his athleticism and break up the attempted pass play. You may be thinking, *Wow! That's not nice.* Who said winning is supposed to be "nice"? Yes, you play by the rules, but sometimes you need to be shrewd.

During quarantine, I have also been reading my Bible, particularly the book of Revelation. Interestingly, I came across a Scripture passage that I must have read hundreds of times during my sixty-five years in church—Luke 16:1–9, the "Parable of the Shrewd Manager." But I have never heard it taught by any pastor like I "heard" it this time when the Holy Spirit downloaded a revelation to me.

You will want to read it for yourself. But in a nutshell, this passage—taught by Jesus Himself to His disciples—tells the story of a wealthy man's manager who was about to be fired for dishonesty. Desperate to hold onto his job, the manager came up with a "shrewd" plan that would both salvage his employment and save most of his employer's money.

OUR GAME PLAN

This unique passage gives us insight into surviving the unexpected, which in the wake of the pandemic, *is to be expected!* But, first, let's be sure we understand the meaning of the word *shrewd.* Contrary to some opinions—that this word suggests the idea of manipulation—Webster gives this additional definition: "practical hard-headed cleverness and judgment."[32] Other versions of the Bible simply use the word *wise.*

So, how can we be wise and discerning about the future, where anything can happen—a layoff from your job, a grim diagnosis from the doctor, a global shutdown? Check out the following game plan and implement these ideas as they apply to your location and your spiritual, physical, and financial needs:

1. **Gather a team of friends, neighbors, family, and trusted advisors.** You could call this your "cluster." It is this cluster of people who will be able to provide wisdom, insight, and even possible provisions should that become necessary. We have recently purchased food that will last twenty years— enough for ourselves, our families, and others who might need it if the situation becomes really desperate.

2. **Pay close attention to Luke 16:8–9:** The master commended the dishonest manager because he had acted shrewdly. For the people of this world are more shrewd in dealing with their own kind than are the people of the light. I tell you, use

worldly wealth to gain friends for yourselves, so that when it is gone, you will be welcomed into eternal dwellings. Some of your friends and neighbors may not necessarily be believers/Christians at the moment, but God often places people in our path who will be mutually beneficial for His purposes. But look out for snakes; watch what people do, not what they say.

3. **Stay invested, diversified, and liquid.** (Refer to Chart 5 at the back of this book.) No matter who wins or loses an election, you can make money in any environment with a competent team (remember your CPA, lawyer, and investment advisor). In tough times, be careful of old-school strategies. You need to reevaluate your investment choices no less than annually. For example: Why buy oil and carbon-related stocks when there is currently a glut on the market? (Remember when Presidents Nixon and Carter thought we would be out of oil by the year 2020? But that could change tomorrow.) Why buy commercial real estate with people working from home? Check out AlphaDEX ETFs that are sector-based. They may have higher fees than other indexed ETFs, but they can provide you with some badly needed juice for your portfolio at the right time. (Your advisory team can guide you.) In early April of 2020, we called most of our customers with more than $100,000 of investable assets and offered to take up to 20% of their monies to purchase triple S&P 500 ETF-hedged position. We took some risk, but it paid off. The average return was over 140% in eighteen weeks! This is called opportunity investing. And yes, one needs to be prudent, but this kind of opportunity doesn't come along every day. The prophet Daniel predicted this technology revolution over 2,500 years ago, so be ready to profit from it (see Daniel 12:4). But don't forget to stay liquid. If/when things get really bad, you may need to

access funds quickly. Keep two years of your RMD for IRA accounts in short-term bond ETFs and enough emergency monies in the local bank to cover your needs—from $5,000 to $25,000, depending upon your individual circumstances.

4. **Keep up to date on tax policy.** As I mentioned in the chapter "Quicksand," my biggest debt—as is true of most successful small business owners—is **taxes!** Not credit cards or mortgages. Either now or in the foreseeable future, we will be faced with tax increases. If the new proposed tax plan is enacted, one of the main changes would be the loss of the "step-up in basis."[33] With an estimated $40 trillion of monies transferred from baby boomers to millennials, the government will want a piece of that action to the tune of 40% of all your assets, excluding your house. If you do the math, you will easily see that's $16 trillion the government will expect your family to pay *in assets and monies that have already been taxed once!* Careful planning with your advisory team can help you avoid this largest tax increase in U.S. history.

As you may know, the new CARES Act increased taxes on all inherited IRA accounts that will pass to the next generation. Children's inherited IRA accounts are now taxed over ten years at ordinary tax rates vs. spread over the children's/beneficiary's lifetime. Here are some strategies to consider:

- Donate your IRA to your church or charity if you don't need it now.
- At age 72—if your portfolio is healthy enough—donate up to $100,000 per year as your RMD to a church or charity. This "qualified charitable distribution" is annual and is in danger of being rescinded.
- Create a Charitable Remainder Unit Trust (CRUT) or Charitable Remainder Annuity Trust (CRAT). (Your

legal team can advise you as to which trust is best for you.) These types of trusts legally protect your assets from capital gains taxes (i.e., especially stepped-up basis, and federal estate taxes when you leave your estate to your family). These trusts can also give you a carry-forward tax deduction as well as an income stream for generations. Only 10% of the principal (or corpus) of the trust goes to charity.

- To secure your real estate, form an LLC with your children. (Depending upon the amount of real estate you own and the number of children, you may need to form a separate LLC for each child.) All fees and expenses related to the house/houses can be paid via the LLC. Children can also allocate monies back to their parents for food and other necessities. Please check with your accountant or eldercare lawyer as each state has its own rules, which can be confusing.

5. **Take care of your physical body.** I try to exercise three times a week—biking, running, stretching, rowing—whatever I can do to stay in shape. Two weekends ago, I ran a 5K in Mohican State Park, at over 1,500 feet elevation. My grandkids love to beat me in soccer, kickball, and flag football. Great way to connect with them. As you might imagine, my business can be extremely stressful—especially with clients losing money during business shutdowns (i.e., COVID-19)! Going for a hike or a walk helps me maintain my perspective. I call these my personal prayer times. I turn off my iPhone. No music. Just me and my Maker.And what about "the vaccine"? Let me put it this way: in my lifetime, I have had pneumonia, rheumatic fever, a brain tumor, foot surgeries, an ablation for atrial fibrillation—and, more recently, COVID-19. Not the worst illness I have experienced. But what if the government mandates that I

have to take the COVID-19 vaccine to shop at Walmart or Target or fly somewhere on vacation? If that happens, it would be a red flag for me. I have some questions about this vaccine. Too many questions. Too few answers. Yes, medical technological advances are a blessing from God, but genetic research can take place without the use of aborted fetal tissue, right? Could my own blood be the cure? Twenty-five hundred years ago, the prophet Daniel predicted that "knowledge shall increase" (12:4).

6.   **Most importantly, PRAY!** But pray with purpose. Ask God to give you divine direction through dreams, visions, and supernatural manifestations that can be confirmed by the Word of God and the testimonies of others. No man's prophetic word ever contradicts God's Word!Bill and Beni Johnson express it best in their devotional book *Mornings and Evenings in His Presence*: "The Bible does not say, 'My people perish for lack of miracles, or lack of money, or because of bad relationships or bad worship leaders or insufficient nursery staff' or anything else we could list. Proverbs 29:18 says: 'Where there is no prophetic revelation, the people cast off restraints.' A more correct and complete translation is, 'Without prophetic revelation, the people go unrestrained, walking in circles, having no certain destiny.'"[34]God's prophetic word does not often come in a sonic boom or a refrain that echoes off the walls of canyons. Instead, it is sometimes nothing more than a gentle nudge or a quiet whisper. But if we ask, He will answer.

HOW MUCH IS ENOUGH?

A few weeks ago, Kim and I spent a few days in Destin, Florida, once again enjoying the warm weather and walks on the beach.

Earlier, my wife had given her okay to purchase some property there for family vacations, preferably beachfront, as well as some condo units for rental purposes. But every time I did the math, I struggled with the HOA fees and other costs. Yes, the income from the rentals would cover most of the expenses, unless hurricanes hit or COVID spiked again. Then, too, interest rates were low, which would make the debt payment reasonable. I would not use my investment assets to purchase a property since they were making way more than the interest costs. Even with all that considered, we had gone so far as to pick out the properties we liked and were ready to make an offer...

When I am questioning a business or personal decision, it is always wise to check with the Owner's Manual—the Bible. Luke highlights a parable that gave me some clarity on this particular decision. It's the "Parable of the Foolish Rich Man" that Jesus shared with His disciples in Luke 12:13–21. When a very wealthy landowner ran out of room to store his grain, he decided to build an even bigger barn, then sit back and *"take life easy; eat, drink, and be merry. But God said to him, 'You fool! This very night your life will be demanded from you. Then who will get what you have prepared for yourself?'"* (v. 20).

Greed is a terrible thing and something we must guard against. On the way home from Florida, I heard a familiar still, small voice saying, *Not now.* My wife confirmed.

Needless to say, Kim and I didn't buy the beachfront property that day. Even if I paid cash, there would still be over $30,000 per year in fees and insurance. We could rent there for two months for that amount, with no risk of hurricane and no investment risk. Then, if a storm swept through, we could simply pack up and go home, leaving the clean-up to someone else! Why did we need more property?[35] Enough is enough.

But there is much more to this story. In the final analysis, the question is: Do you possess your "stuff" or does your "stuff" possess you? Or have you learned what really matters? Your *true* net worth...and how to build it...for now and forever. Have you consulted the Wise Counselor?

Have You Consulted the Wise Counselor?
(Luke 24:13–35, author paraphrase)

"Is it true? Is it over? Is he really gone?"

The man's traveling companion nodded sadly. "I'm afraid so. And just when we thought we had found the one who could bring us justice and rescue us from this evil tyranny."

They had not expected this outcome. There were no words to describe their grief, their despair.

The two walked on down the dusty road in silence, the jeers of the mocking crowd still ringing in their ears. The hollow sound of the spikes driven into a cruel Roman cross—penetrating innocent human flesh. The agonized cries of two robbers, also impaled. The final, gasping breath of the one they had followed faithfully for three years.

So steeped in their own hopelessness were they that they barely noticed a fellow traveler who had joined them on their trek toward home after the execution and burial of their friend and Master.

He spoke quietly, asking, "Why so sad and gloomy?"

"Haven't you heard?" The first was shocked. "Are you the only person around who hasn't heard what has been going on the last few days?"

"Tell me."

The words of the two tumbled over each other as they shared with this stranger all that had taken place. The armed military in the Garden of Gethsemane. The fake trial. The sham verdict. The crucifixion. The quake that had violently shaken the earth with His last breath.

They walked on while their companion began talking. "Beginning with Moses and all the prophets, he carefully unveiled to them the revelation of himself throughout the Scriptures."

When they reached their village, and still not fully understanding, they begged Him to stay with them a while longer. Only as He broke bread with them at their table did they recognize Jesus. Only then could they grasp that He had fed them with Living Bread as they walked together. Only now was He fully revealed to them—the Son of God, their Hope, their Deliverer. Everything they needed. Everything they had longed for.

It had been only hours since His resurrection, yet Jesus knew the pain of these two and had come to them with answers to all their questions. They lived in a hostile environment under the rule of a foreign government. They had no idea what would happen next. It was very possible that they, too, would be arrested, tortured, killed. Knowing their fear, Jesus met them where they were—on the dusty road to Emmaus. He quieted their hearts and gave them reason to believe again.

We are like those two disciples with our fears and our anxious thoughts. Our world, too, is in chaos. What will happen next? Could we survive a stock market crash, another COVID-19? Only He knows—the ultimate Wise Counselor. And just as Jesus came to them, He comes to us on *our* dusty road, offering revelation for our journey.

WHATEVER HAPPENS: "FEAR NOT!"

I am not saying we should disregard historic events. I am a patriotic citizen of the greatest country in the world. Nor am I saying we should dismiss the seriousness of pandemics. I know that firsthand. What I am saying is that *fear is an emotion that can blind us to the truth.*

Many people—believers and non-believers alike—spend thousands of dollars each year on fear-based literature. The best-selling book in 1970 was *The Late Great Planet Earth* by Hal Lindsay, who predicted the end of the world within five years of that date. Lindsay, of course, was 100% wrong! Remember all the books predicting a coming economic earthquake at the turn of the century, the millennial year 2000? Didn't happen. Remember the book *88 Reasons Why the Rapture Will Be in 1988* by Edgar C. Whisenant? Obviously, that didn't happen either. Most of those books were based on one word—FEAR. Publishers sold millions of copies of books and made the authors wealthy, but the earth didn't quake. The destruction of America at Y2K, the turn of the 21st century? Wrong again. And the most recent pandemic? Not nearly as deadly as many would have us believe.

Supposedly, such "prophets" have a unique perspective. Yet, when their "prophecies" are proven inaccurate, few are held accountable for their fearmongering that, incidentally, makes them lots of money. There is certainly a place for the prophetic in our world. But true prophets are known by their good fruit. They hear from God and faithfully relay what they have heard to others.

Is this the last generation before the Lord returns? Well, I don't have the answer to that, but I do know that this will be *your* last generation—and *mine.* I do not profess to be a prophet, but let's look at a story that was written 3,500 years ago when Moses sent twelve spies into the Land of Promise (see Numbers 13:1–33.) Ten of the spies came back with a nay-saying report that caused the hearts of the people to melt, just as bad news today—CNN, MSNBC, *New York Times, The Washington Post,* etc.—can cause people to live in constant fear and inhibit them from seizing the opportunities before them.

In the swirl of politics and pandemics, one clear voice echoes over 2,000 years of biblical history: "Fear not!" At least 365 times in God's Word—one announcement for each day of the year—we read that we are not to be afraid. "Fear not!" He says...

- To the shepherds tending their flocks on the night of Jesus' birth.
- To the frightened disciples on the stormy Sea of Galilee.
- To the two on the road to Emmaus.
- To the women at the tomb on the first Resurrection morning.

And to all of us—today—caught in the dark web of the battle between good and evil: "Fear not!"

Within the Bible, as I have mentioned, is recorded over two thousand references to wealth and how we are to steward it while on earth. Based on that timeless truth, I can condense my book into a few simple concepts: *Work. Save. Invest. Give. Share.* It's as simple as that. But whatever happens, don't be afraid. If you have secured equity in heaven, the best is yet to come!

But don't stop after you finish this chapter. Turn the page and complete your simple action plan. Also, to learn more about actions you can take to grow and protect your net worth, see the additional resources at BuildYourTrueNetWorth.com.

Bottom Line: *Be open to hear, see, and discern the truth because the truth will set you free. Free from fear! Free from failure! Free from futility!*

SIMPLE ACTION PLAN

Complete the following ten steps.

1. Stop procrastinating or trying to find the perfect investment and start investing now.
2. Search the internet for "simple budget form," and complete it as best as you can. Remember that your budget will change periodically based lifestyle needs and desires.
3. Determine your current net worth using the worksheet in Appendix A.
4. Remember to pay yourself first—a minimum of $50 per month (see Chart 1). You need at least $250 to open the account with most institutions. Make sure your investing is automated (ACH withdrawal from your checking account into a brokerage account, individual or joint) so the money comes out of your account directly without you having to think about it or do it yourself. Places to invest include:
   - Your 401(k) plan
   - A company match on your 401(k) plan
   - Your Roth IRA account if you qualify
   - Acorns account (some banks allow you to round up to the nearest dollar for each financial transaction and then invest the money into one of the Acorns portfolios)

5. Complete a will because if you don't, the state you live in has one for you, which you do not want

6. Get life insurance
   - How much? The standard recommendation is 10 times your annual income
   - What kind? Term insurance insures you for a set number of years. Whole life insures you for life. I suggest both.

7. Start a business you've dreamed about
   - The number one hindrance is usually lack of capital. See chapter 7 for practical ways to raise money to start your business.
   - Do your research and create a marketing plan so you know your product well and who you can sell it to.
   - Be sure to keep your priorities balanced between work and play.
   - Follow government regulations and hire experts to help you follow the law

8. Remember that you have not because you have not asked. Ask God and others for advice and wisdom! (See James 4:2–3.)

9. Find a great independent Financial Advisor in your area who will help you with a financial plan. (If you would like to work with us and have over $250,000 of investable assets, we would be glad to walk you through our 5D process. Go to BuildYourTrueNetWorth.com to complete a disclosure form.)

10. Read #1 again and remember it's not the amount of money invested but the amount of time your money is invested. Opportunities are everywhere. You just have to look for them.

CHARTS

CHART 1

Illustration of Hypothetical Mutual Fund Growth of $50 per Month

Important Disclosures

Figures shown are past results and are not predictive of results in future periods. Current and future results may be lower or higher than those shown. Share prices and returns will vary, so investors may lose money. Investing for short periods makes losses more likely. For more current information and month-end results, visit capitalgroup.com.

Investors should carefully consider investment objectives, risks, charges and expenses. This and other important information is contained in the fund prospectuses, summary prospectuses, CollegeAmerica Program Description and ABLEAmerica Program Description, which should be obtained from a financial professional and should be read carefully before investing.

Regular investing does not ensure a profit or protect against loss. Market indexes are unmanaged and, therefore, have no expenses. Investors cannot invest directly in an index. Results for the Lipper indexes do not reflect sales charges. There have been periods when the fund has lagged the index.

This illustration must be preceded or accompanied by the fund's current summary prospectus or prospectus, which details charges, expenses, investment objectives and operating policies. American Funds Distributors, Inc., member FINRA.

Investment results assume all distributions are reinvested and reflect applicable fees and expenses. Expense ratios are as of each fund's prospectus available at the time of publication. For the funds and/ or share classes listed below, the investment adviser is currently reimbursing a portion of the funds' fees or expenses, without which the results would have been lower and net expense ratios higher.

· American Funds Corporate Bond Fund: all share classes (through at least 8/1/20).
· American Funds Tax-Exempt Fund of New York: all share classes (through at least 10/1/20).
· American Funds Mortgage Fund: Class R-2E and R-5E shares (through at least 11/1/20).
· Short-Term Bond Fund of America: Class F-3 shares (through at least 11/1/20).
· American Funds Retirement Income Portfolio - Conservative: Class R-2E and R-5 shares (through at least 1/1/21).
· American Funds Retirement Income Portfolio - Moderate: Class R-5E, R-5 and R-6 (through at least 1/1/21).
· American Funds Retirement Income Portfolio - Enhanced: Class R-5 and R-6 shares (through at least 1/1/21).
· American Funds Preservation Portfolio: Class R-2E shares (through at least 1/1/21).
· American Funds Tax-Exempt Preservation Portfolio: all share classes (through at least 1/1/21).

The investment adviser may elect at its discretion to extend, modify or terminate the reimbursements at that time. Please see each fund's most recent prospectus for details.

For the funds listed below, the fund's transfer agent is currently waiving a portion of the funds' other expenses, without which the results would have been lower and net expense ratios higher.

· American Funds Developing World Growth and Income Fund and American Funds Inflation Linked Bond Fund: Class F-3 shares (through at least 2/1/21).

The transfer agent may elect at its discretion to extend, modify or terminate the waiver at that time. Please see each fund's most recent prospectus for details.

Virginia529℠, as program administrator of ABLEAmerica, is currently waiving the fee owed to it as compensation for its oversight and administration of ABLEAmerica. This waiver will be in effect for Class ABLE-A shares through at least December 1, 2019 for American Funds U.S. Government Money Market Fund and January 1, 2020 for the Portfolio Fund Series. Subject to the terms of its contractual arrangement with the investment adviser, Virginia529℠ may elect to extend, modify or terminate the waiver at that time.

Standardized Average Annual Total Returns for Quarter Ended 12/31/2020
Returns for periods of less than one year are not annualized

Hypothetical Illustration

Inception Max. Initial Sales

Security Name	Inception Date	Max. Initial Sales Charge/ CDSC	1 Year	5 Years	10 Years	Since Inception
The Growth Fund of America A (AGTHX)	12/1/1973	5.75% Front	29.89%	17.20%	14.59%	13.91%

Gross Charges and Expenses

Fund Name	Sales Charge	Max CDSC	Max Redem Fee	Total Gross Operating Expense
The Growth Fund of America A (AGTHX)	5.75%	1.00%	0.00%	0.64%

The fund does not assess redemption fees. However, shareholders redeeming shares may be subject to the fund's Purchase Blocking Policy as described in the prospectus.

The illustration included herein does not reflect the effects of taxes in some or all of the investments.

- Cumulative Volume Discount Reflected Where Applicable in This Illustration.
- NOTE: Systematic Accumulation Plans cannot assure a profit or protect against loss in declining markets.

Class A shares are subject to an up-front maximum sales charge of 5.75% for equity, Target Date, Retirement Income and most Portfolio Series funds, 3.75% for most fixed income funds and American Funds Tax-Aware Conservative Growth and Income Portfolio, and 2.50% for Intermediate Bond Fund of America, Short-Term Bond Fund of America, American Funds Short-Term Tax-Exempt Bond Fund, Limited Term Tax-Exempt Bond Fund of America, American Funds Preservation Portfolio and American Funds Tax-Exempt Preservation Portfolio. Data prior to 6/30/2020, returns reflect deduction of the maximum sales charge: 5.75% for equity funds and most Portfolio Series funds and 3.75% for most fixed income funds maximum sales charges. The sales charge declines for accounts and aggregated investments ($25,000 for equity and target date funds, $100,000 for most bond funds, $500,000 for Intermediate Bond Fund of America, Short Term Bond Fund of America, Ameridan Funds Short-Term Tax-Exempt Bond Fund, and Limited Term Tax-Exempt Bond Fund of America). There is no initial sales charge on purchases of $1 million or more. A 1% contingent deferred sales charge (CDSC) may be assessed if a redemption occurs within 18 months of purchase. Results on the following pages reflect deduction of the CDSC if the investment is $1 million or more and a withdrawal is selected within 18 months of purchase. Certain withdrawals before age 59 1/2 may be subject to income tax and, if applicable, to a 10% federal penalty.

- The A/529-A share 1, 5, and 10-year return for each fund is based on the MOP value.
- The "Average annual return on the investment" is based on the initial investment and the breakpoint chosen.

If the results shown on the following pages do not reflect deduction of an initial sales charge (i.e. they are at net asset value), please note that they would have been lower if the sales charge had been deducted.

Investing outside the United States involves additional risks, such as currency fluctuations, periods of illiquidity and price volatility, as more fully described in the prospectus. These risks may be heightened in connection with investments in developing countries.

Hypothetical Illustration

The Growth Fund of America A (AGTHX)

Date	Initial Investment	Initial Sales Charge	Net Amount Invested	Shares Purchased
12/01/1973	$250.00	5.75%	$235	163.399

$250 initial investment on 12/01/1973. Dividends and capital gains are reinvested. Subsequent investments of $50.00 from 01/01/1974 to 12/30/2020 every month, on the last day of the month. The initial investment is subject to a 5.75% sales charge. Subsequent investments are subject to a sales charge of up to 5.75%. The effects of income and capital gains taxes are not demonstrated.

Date	Investment(s)	Dividend Income	Total Dividend Income	Capital Gains	Shares Held	Total Value
12/31/1973	250	0	0	0	163	236
12/31/1974	600	28	28	0	624	672
12/31/1975	600	34	63	0	1,052	1,496
12/31/1976	600	7	69	0	1,403	2,351
12/31/1977	600	18	87	0	1,741	3,478
12/31/1978	600	47	135	0	2,003	5,024
12/31/1979	600	92	227	0	2,223	8,015
12/31/1980	600	175	402	0	2,402	11,916
12/31/1981	600	561	963	0	2,644	12,533
12/31/1982	600	806	1,769	0	2,918	16,383
12/31/1983	600	596	2,365	403	3,148	21,377
12/31/1984	600	466	2,832	177	3,348	20,773
12/31/1985	600	375	3,207	1,483	3,725	27,025
12/31/1986	600	529	3,735	1,492	4,057	31,970
12/31/1987	600	595	4,331	2,290	4,476	34,826
12/31/1988	600	703	5,034	1,338	4,780	41,850
12/31/1989	600	1,473	6,507	4,806	5,458	55,043
12/31/1990	600	1,323	7,830	2,260	5,921	53,349
12/31/1991	600	1,045	8,874	3,194	6,374	73,083
12/31/1992	600	610	9,484	289	6,500	79,109
12/31/1993	600	392	9,877	3,172	6,818	91,194
12/31/1994	600	583	10,460	3,566	7,191	91,791

Hypothetical Illustration

Date	Investment(s)	Dividend Income	Total Dividend Income	Capital Gains	Shares Held	Total Value
12/31/1995	600	1,048	11,508	8,201	7,844	119,771
12/31/1996	600	866	12,374	6,774	8,339	138,170
12/31/1997	600	1,088	13,462	17,236	9,367	175,920
12/31/1998	600	845	14,307	20,759	10,380	232,515
12/31/1999	600	468	14,775	33,231	11,651	339,507
12/31/2000	600	1,692	16,467	47,777	13,496	365,483
12/31/2001	600	608	17,075	0	13,547	321,194
12/31/2002	600	258	17,333	0	13,589	250,998
12/31/2003	600	83	17,416	0	13,621	334,259
12/31/2004	600	1,228	18,644	0	13,690	374,835
12/31/2005	600	2,605	21,249	3,085	13,895	428,809
12/31/2006	600	3,810	25,059	15,303	14,492	476,349
12/31/2007	600	5,212	30,272	29,841	15,558	529,119
12/31/2008	600	3,645	33,916	0	15,763	322,820
12/31/2009	600	3,328	37,244	0	15,911	434,842
12/31/2010	600	3,903	41,147	0	16,061	488,891
12/31/2011	600	3,521	44,668	0	16,204	465,534
12/31/2012	600	4,590	49,259	0	16,355	561,790
12/31/2013	600	2,251	51,509	44,981	17,495	752,299
12/31/2014	600	2,941	54,451	71,027	19,281	822,899
12/31/2015	600	5,257	59,708	65,422	21,013	867,625
12/31/2016	600	5,265	64,973	53,179	22,398	941,617
12/31/2017	600	5,602	70,575	72,473	23,989	1,188,408
12/31/2018	600	7,320	77,895	115,676	27,004	1,154,687
12/31/2019	600	10,266	88,161	88,474	28,948	1,480,088
12/31/2020	550	4,923	93,084	79,199	30,210	2,040,409
Total	**28,400**	**93,084**	**93,084**	**797,107**	**30,210**	**2,040,409**

Average annual return on the investment for the period 12/01/1973 - 12/31/2020 : 13.70%

CHART 2
S&P 500 Dividend Yield

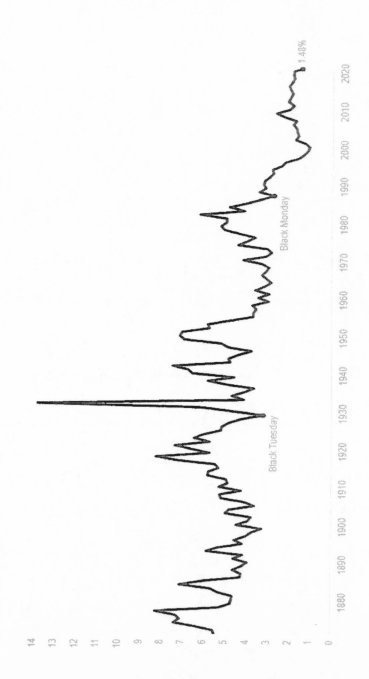

Chart   Table

Current Yield: 1.48% -1.72 bps

3:58 PM EST, Wed Feb 24

Mean:	4.31%	
Median:	4.26%	
Min:	1.11%	(Aug 2000)
Max:	13.84%	(Jun 1932)

S&P 500 dividend yield — (12 month dividend per share)/price.

Yields following December 2020 (including the current yield) are estimated based on 12 month dividends through December 2020, as reported by S&P.

Sources:

o Standard & Poor's for current S&P 500 Dividend Yield.

o Robert Shiller and his book Irrational Exuberance for historic S&P 500 Dividend Yields.

CHART 3
Apple Stock Growth for the Last Five Years

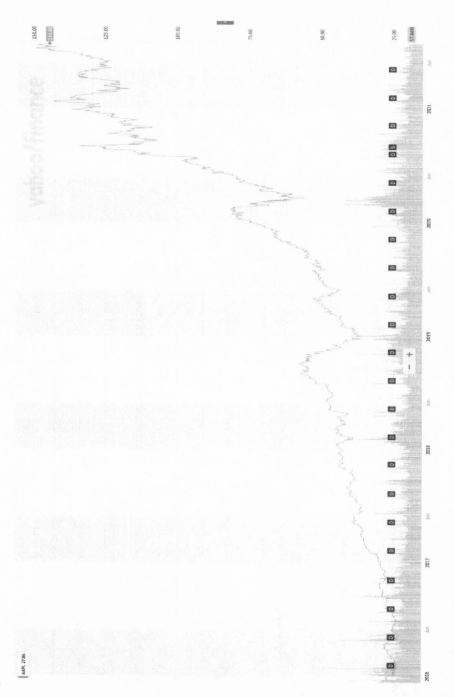

CHART 4
Historical Chart Data for Market Indices

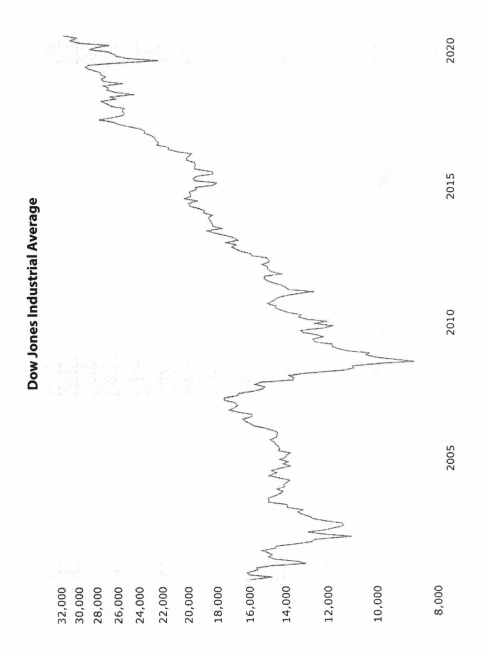

S&P 500

Nasdaq

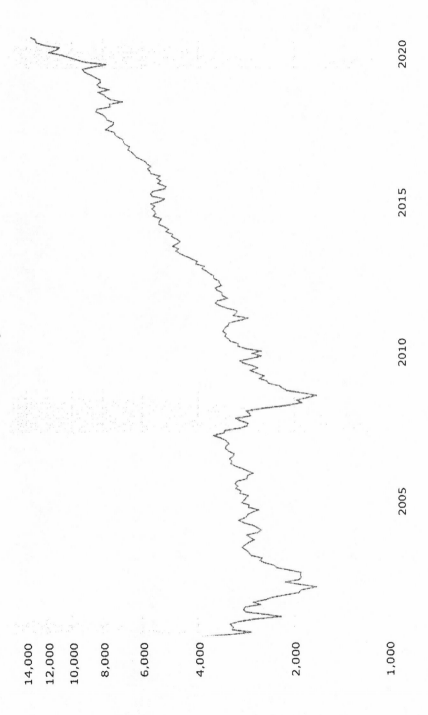

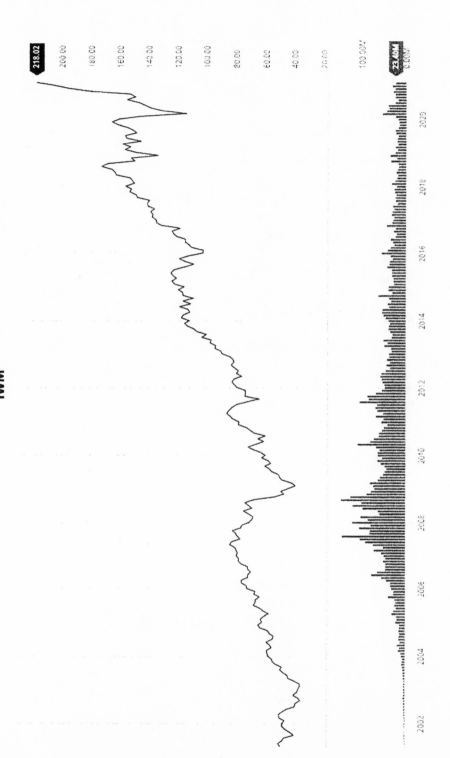

IWM

CHART 5
Impact of Political Parties on Markets

IMPACT OF POLITICAL PARTIES ON MARKETS

Presidential Party	S&P 500 Return	10 Year Yield
Republican	5.5%	-0.36%
Democratic	12.7%	0.21%

Party-Line Control	S&P 500 Return	10 Year Yield
Split	8.2%	-0.27%
Single Party	9.0%	0.24%

Source: Bloomberg, S&P 500 Price Index, 10 Year U.S. Treasury Yield, Data yearly since 1972, 2020 data through 7/31/2020, calculations by Horizon Investments

S&P 500 Index Total Returns: First Year of a Four-Year Presidential Term

Democrat (Average S&P 500 Return: 19.0%) Republican (Average S&P 500 Return: 12.2%)

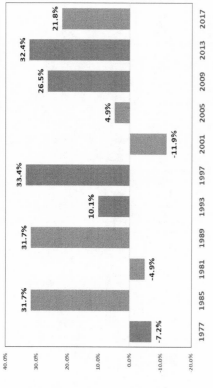

How Stocks Have Fared in the First Year of a Four-Year Presidential Term

S&P 500 Index & Sector Index Total Returns

	1997	2001	2005	2009	2013	2017
White House	Democrat	Republican	Republican	Democrat	Democrat	Republican
Senate	Republican	Democrat	Republican	Democrat	Democrat	Republican
House of Representatives	Republican	Republican	Republican	Democrat	Republican	Republican
S&P 500 Index	33.36%	-11.89%	4.91%	26.46%	32.39%	21.83%
Communication Services	41.02%	-12.43%	-5.71%	8.73%	11.59%	-1.66%
Consumer Discretionary	33.19%	-1.15%	-4.78%	43.44%	43.27%	22.51%
Consumer Staples	33.46%	-4.77%	3.92%	15.29%	26.79%	13.10%
Energy	24.66%	-11.19%	33.76%	16.41%	25.39%	-2.05%
Financials	51.23%	-8.03%	6.58%	15.48%	34.25%	20.89%
Health Care	38.99%	-11.11%	7.49%	20.76%	42.19%	22.47%
Industrials	26.56%	-5.20%	3.78%	21.68%	41.19%	21.06%
Information Technology	26.92%	-24.16%	1.58%	61.04%	28.99%	37.29%
Materials	10.03%	4.60%	4.50%	49.74%	26.02%	22.66%
Utilities	26.51%	-26.69%	15.21%	12.79%	15.08%	12.16%

APPENDIX A

Current Net Worth Worksheet

PERSONAL FINANCIAL STATEMENT

NAME(S): _____   ☐ Individual   ☐ Joint with Spouse

ASSETS	DOLLARS	LIABILITIES	DOLLARS
Cash, Savings Accounts and CDs		Credit Card Balances	
Retirement Accounts (IRA, 401K, etc.)		Automobile Loans	
Stocks & Bonds not held in Retirement Accounts		Notes Payable-Business(es) Owned	
Accounts and Notes Receivable		Notes Payable to Others	
Real Estate Owned-From Schedule		Other Unpaid Taxes and Interest	
Automobiles and other Personal Property		Real Estate Mortgages Payable-From Schedule	
Business(es): 1.		Other Liabilities: 1.	
2.		2.	
3.		3.	
Other Assets: 1.			
2.		TOTAL LIABILITIES	
		NET WORTH (Assets minus Liabilities)	
TOTAL ASSETS		TOTAL LIABILITIES AND NET WORTH	

SCHEDULE OF REAL ESTATE OWNED

Property Address	Title In Name of	Date Acquired	Original Cost	Present Market Value	Mortgage Information		
					Balance	Maturity	Mortgage Holder
			Totals				

SOURCE OF INCOME	DOLLARS	CONTINGENT LIABILITIES	DOLLARS
Salary		As Endorser, Co-Maker or Guarantor	
Net Investment Income		Legal Claims & Judgments	
Other Income (Describe Below) You need not disclose income from alimony, child support, or separate mainte-nance unless you wish such amount to be considered in the credit determina-tion.		Provision for Federal Income Tax	
Description of Other Income			

APPENDIX B
Recommended Reading List

Cathy, S. Truett. *Wealth, Is It Worth It?* Decatur, Georgia: Looking Glass Books, Inc., 2011.

Colson, Chuck and Jack Eckerd. *Why America Doesn't Work.* Dallas, Texas: Word Publishing, 1991.

Owens, Candace. *Blackout: How Black America Can Make Its Second Escape from the Democrat Plantation.* Avon, Massachusetts: Simon & Schuster, 2020.

Payne, Charles. *Unstoppable Prosperity: Learn the Strategy I've Used to Beat the Market Every Year.* Boulder, Colorado: Paradigm Direct, LLC, 2019.

Ramsey, Dave. *The Total Money Makeover.* Nashville: Thomas Nelson Publishers, 2003.

Robinson, Mickey. *Supernatural Courage: Activating Spiritual Bravery to Win Today's Battle.* Bloomington, Minnesota: Chosen Books, 2020.

Siegel, Jeremy J. *Stocks for the Long Run: The Definitive Guide to Financial Market Returns and Long-Term Investment Strategies.* New York: McGraw Hill Education, 2014, 2008, 2002, 1998,1994.

Smith, Jason L. *The Bucket Plan®: Protecting and Growing Your Assets for a Worry-Free Retirement.* Austin, Texas: Greenleaf Book Group Press, 2017.

APPENDIX C
A Biblical View for Building Your True Net Worth

A good man leaves an inheritance for his children's
children,
but a sinner's wealth is stored up for the righteous.
(Proverbs 13:22)

The plans of the diligent lead to profit
as surely as haste leads to poverty.
(Proverbs 21:5)

A generous man will himself be blessed,
for he shares his food with the poor.
(Proverbs 22:9)

THE PARABLE OF THE TALENTS
(Matthew 25:14–30)

"Again, it will be like a man going on a journey, who called
his servants and entrusted his property to them. To one he
gave five talents of money, to another two talents, and to
another one talent, each according to his own ability. Then
he went on his journey. The man who had received the five
talents went at once and put his money to work and gained
five more. So also, the one with the two talents gained two
more. But the man who had received the one talent went off,
dug a hole in the ground and hid his master's money.

"After a long time the master of those servants returned
and settled accounts with them. The man who had received
the five talents brought the other five. 'Master,' he said, 'you
entrusted me with five talents. See, I have gained five more.'

"His master replied, 'Well done, good and faithful servant! You have been faithful with a few things; I will put you in charge of many things. Come and share your master's happiness!'

"The man with the two talents also came. 'Master,' he said, 'you entrusted me with two talents; see, I have gained two more.'

"His master replied, 'Well done, good and faithful servant! You have been faithful with a few things; I will put you in charge of many things. Come and share your master's happiness!'

"Then the man who had received the one talent came. 'Master,' he said, 'I knew that you are a hard man, harvesting where you have not sown and gathering where you have not scattered seed. So I was afraid and went out and hid your talent in the ground. See, here is what belongs to you.'

"His master replied, 'You wicked, lazy servant! So you knew that I harvest where I have not sown and gather where I have not scattered seed? Well then, you should have put my money on deposit with the bankers, so that when I returned I would have received it back with interest.

"'Take the talent from him and give it to the one who has the ten talents. For everyone who has will be given more, and he will have an abundance. Whoever does not have, even what he has will be taken from him. And throw that worthless servant outside, into the darkness, where there will be weeping and gnashing of teeth.'"

THE TRUSTWORTHY SERVANT
Luke 16:10–13

"Whoever can be trusted with very little can also be trusted with much, and whoever is dishonest with very little will also be dishonest with much. So if you have not been trustworthy in handling worldly wealth, who will trust you with true riches? And if you have not been trustworthy with someone else's property, who will give you property of your own?

"No servant can serve two masters. Either he will hate the one and love the other, or he will be devoted to the one and despise the other. You cannot serve both God and money."

AN INHERITANCE THAT LASTS
I Peter 1:3-7

"Praise be to the God and Father of our Lord Jesus Christ! In his great mercy he has given us new birth into a living hope through the resurrection of Jesus Christ from the dead, and into an inheritance that can never perish, spoil, or fade—kept in heaven for you, who through faith are shielded by God's power until the coming of the salvation that is ready to be revealed in the last time.

In this you greatly rejoice, though now for a little while you may have had to suffer grief in all kinds of trials. These have come so that your faith—of greater worth than gold, which perishes even though refined by fire—may be proved genuine and may result in praise, glory and honor when Jesus Christ is revealed."

ACKNOWLEDGMENTS

As I have stated in my book dedication without My Mother and my wife I would probably be sitting in some jail today or even worse, a prisoner within my own insecurities.

Mickey Robinson is a truly unique individual and together with his wife Barbara have been a constant encouragement for me to write and finish this book. Our families have a long relationship going back over 30 years when we vacationed together in Georgian Bay, Canada. One quick story. The first time we drove there, was what I would consider a trip to hell. Just north of Toronto, we get stuck in a traffic jam for several hours. Shortly after we get through that we have a flat tire on the trailer hauling the boat we took to fish out of. And if that wasn't enough to get your heart beating fast. We unload all our gear into the cabin after 16 hours on the road with my four children and his four in two separate vans. Just a tad stressful to say the least. The last thing we unload is our fishing poles and somehow a hook gets caught in Mickey's thumb and inadvertently Jacob, Mickey's middle son trips over the fishing line and buries it into his thumb past the barb. So off to the emergency room two hours away. A twenty-hour hour day. Vacation is supposed to be relaxing!!!!!!

If you want to get to know someone you either must work with them, vacation with them, or have them live in your house. Oh the fourth thing, play golf with them.

Mickey introduced me to Ann Severance, whom we, Kim, and I count as a privilege to work with as my Ghostwriter. When we first talked to her on the phone Kim and I both could not believe she was 84 years young. She has inspired me so much that I am working on my second book. And I just recently told her she has to live another ten years to help write the revisions to this book. One chapter in the book is dedicated to her" why retirement isn't in the Bible". As we proceeded on this journey it became evident that God had orchestrated this collaboration. I received a D in creative writing at Otterbein University. My only D in college. So that should give you some indication of how valuable she is to this project. Thank you, Ann.

To David Sluka and his team. Thank you.

KYLE E. BEVERIDGE is president of ESB W&I (Wealth and Investments). He began his career with E.S. Beveridge & Associates in 1978, immediately after graduating from Otterbein University. Starting out as a sales rep of life and health insurance, Mr. Beveridge transitioned into sales and consultation of pension plans/401(k) plans.

In 1983, Mr. Beveridge assumed control of E.S. Beveridge & Associates, with gross sales of $100,000 and one part-time employee. By 2000, the company had gained over one hundred 401(k) plans and eleven full-time employees.

In 2012, E.S. Beveridge & Associates was split, forming three new entities: ESB Wealth Management (401(k) plans, ProTPA, and ESB Investments, Inc. [personal investments], with E.S. Beveridge & Associates remaining to focus on health care insurance. Additionally, in 2012, ESB Wealth purchased a 401(k) book of business in Seattle and Tacoma, Washington.

Today, with several great sales reps and technology to match, plus a new name—ESB W&I (Wealth and Investments)—he is transitioning from marketing 401(k) plans to individual planning and 401(k) plans, the reverse of the company's strategy for the past thirty years. ESB W&I will continue to expand in several states, always looking to add quality sales reps to the team.

Mr. Beveridge now devotes the majority of his working time to ESB W&I, focusing on portfolio management, retirement planning, and succession planning. When he is not involved with his clients, he invests in his family, as he enjoys traveling with his wife, Kim, working on the farm, golfing, and spending time with his four children and ten grandchildren.

*Please visit **www.buildyourtruenetworth.com** for helpful resources from Kyle and to learn more about how you can build your true net worth.*

ENDNOTES

1 Sheryl Nance-Nash, "Is the Bible the Ultimate Financial Guide?" Forbes Woman, May 24, 2012, forbes.com/sites/sherylnancenash/2012/05/24/is-the-bible-the-ultimate-financial-guide/?sh=7515e1fc6493.

2 Used by permission of the author, Ann Platz Groton, from her blog "Pray Big."

3 Bennett Lowenthal, "The Jumpers of '29," Washington Post, October 25, 1987, https://www.washingtonpost.com/archive/opinions/1987/10/25/the-jumpers-of-29/17defff9-f725-43b7-831b-7924ac0a1363/.

4 "Net worth," Bankrate.com, https://www.bankrate.com/glossary/n/net-worth/#:~:text=Net%20worth%20is%20a%20measure,minus%20any%20obligations%20or%20liabilities.

5 Tony Dungy, Quiet Strength (Carol Stream, Illinois: Tyndale Momentum, 2007), 317.

6: Don Daszkowski, "Ray Kroc and the McDonald's Phenomenon," The Balance, September 24, 2018, https://www.thebalancesmb.com/the-ray-kroc-story-mcdonalds-facts-and-history-1350971.

7: "McDonald's Vision and Mission Statement Analysis," Mission Statement, http://mission-statement.com/mcdonalds/.

8: Lisa Napoli, "Meet the Woman Who Gave Away the McDonald's Founder's Fortune," Time, December 22, 2016, https://time.com/4616956/mcdonalds-founder-ray-kroc-joan-kroc/.

9: Mike Lindell, What Are the Odds?: From Crack Addict to CEO (Chaska, Minnesota: Lindell Publishing, 2019), from the Foreword by Dr. Ben Carson.

10: S. Truett Cathy, Wealth: Is it Worth It? (Decatur, Georgia: Looking Glass Books, Inc., 2011).

11 Siegel, 289.

12 Jeremy J. Siegel, Stocks for the Long Run (New York: McGraw Hill, 2014, 2008, 2002, 1998, 1994), Preface.

13 Meir Statman, "5 Myths About Stock Diversification," Wall Street Journal, August 8, 2020, http://online.wsj.com

14 Milton Friedman, Capitalism and Freedom (Chicago: The University of Chicago Press, 1962, 1982, 2002), 9.

15 Eric Rosenberg, "Large Cap vs. Mid Cap vs. Small Cap Stocks—Balance Your Portfolio for the Long Run," August 3, 2020, https://investorjunkie.com/investing/small-vs-mid-vs-large-cap-stocks/.

16 Siegel, 272.

17 Adapted from Eric Rosenberg, MBA, "Pros and Cons of Buy Here-Pay Here Dealerships," Self, February 2020, https://www.self.inc/blog/pros-and-cons-of-buy-here-pay-here-car-dealerships.

18 Dave Ramsey, The Money Answer Book (Nashville, Tennessee: Thomas Nelson, 2004), 17.

19 Mark Hall, "The Greatest Wealth Transfer in History: What's Happening and What Are the Implications," Forbes, November 11, 2019, https://www.forbes.com/sites/markhall/2019/11/11/the-greatest-wealth-transfer-in-history-whats-happening-and-what-are-the-implications/.

20 Chuck Colson and Jack Eckerd, Why America Doesn't Work (Dallas: Word Publishers, 1991), 177–178.

21 "New Report Finds 40 Percent of Older Americans Rely Solely on Social Security for Retirement Income," Cision, PR Newswire, https://www.prnewswire.com/news-releases/new-report-finds-

40-percent-of-older-americans-rely-solely-on-social-security-for-retirement-income-300986269.html.

22 "The Average Retirement Savings by Age Group," The Street, updated February 11, 2020, https://www.thestreet.com/retirement/average-retirement-savings-14881067.

23 Jason L. Smith, The Bucket Plan®: Protecting and Growing Your Assets for a Worry-Free Retirement (Austin, Texas: Greenleaf Book Group Press, 2017).

24 "A Beginner's Guide to Understanding 401K," Lonestar Capital Bank, https://www.lscb.com/2019/05/13/a-beginners-guide-to-understanding-401k/.

25 Adapted from Cheryl Winokur Munk, "If You Need Cash Now, Here's Which Account You Should Tap First," Wall Street Journal, August 8, 2020, https://www.wsj.com/articles/if-you-need-cash-now-heres-which-accounts-you-should-tap-first-11596880800.

26 Cathy, Wealth: Is It Worth It?, 8.

27 Ibid., 31.

28 Jean Maalouf, Mother Teresa Essential Writings (Maryknoll: Orbis Books, 2001).

29 Milton Friedman, Capitalism and Freedom (Chicago: University of Chicago Press, 1962, 1982, 2002), 9.

30 From "Word Wealth," New Spirit Filled Life Bible, New King James Version (Nashville: Thomas Nelson Bibles, 2002), 1335. Based on Strong's Concordance, #5278, from the Greek translation of hupomeno.

31 "How Much Might Judas' 30 Pieces of Silver Be Worth Today?" Catholic Share, https://www.catholicshare.com/how-much-might-judas-30-pieces-of-silver-be-worth-today/.

32 Merriam Webster, Merriam-Webster's Collegiate Dictionary, Eleventh Edition (Springfield, Massachusetts: Merriam-Webster, Incorporated, 2006), 1154.

33 "Step-Up in Basis," Investopedia, February 16, 2021, https://www.investopedia.com/terms/s/stepupinbasis.asp.

34 Bill and Beni Johnson, Mornings and Evenings in His Presence (Shippensburg, PA: Destiny Image Publishers, Inc., 2020), 15.

35 See Leo Tolstoy, How Much Land Does a Man Need? (McLean, Virginia: The Trinity Forum, 1996, 2005, 2007).